Advance Praise for

People Tools for Business: 50 Strategies for Building Success, Creating Wealth, and Finding Happiness

"We all want to be happy and successful at work and in our lives . . . Alan Fox shares invaluable insights that can help you make a career out of being happy."

—Tony Hsieh
CEO of Zappos.com, Inc. and author of *Delivering Happiness*

"With refreshing candor, Alan Fox shares the invaluable lessons that he has garnered over an extremely successful, forty-five-year career."

—Brent Kessel
CEO, Abacus Wealth Partners and author of *It's Not About the Money*

"Wise and playful. These charmingly straightforward and practical tools will assist you and add joy to your business life."

—Jack Kornfield
Psychologist, author, and founder of Spirit Rock Meditation Center

"Read this book—it's like having a long, satisfying conversation with your own professional mentor (and mine), Alan Fox."

—Jill E. Fox
From the foreword to *People Tools for Business*

Praise for Alan C. Fox's *New York Times* Best Seller
People Tools: 54 Strategies for Building Relationships, Creating Joy, and Embracing Prosperity

"This book will change your life."
—**Bill Cosby**

"Alan Fox has great tools for emotional intelligence, wisdom, clarity and directness. Develop and use them to live well, and your life will grow better for it."
—**Jack Kornfield**
Psychologist, author, and founder of Spirit Rock Meditation Center

"*People Tools* is a gem of down-to-earth, practical advice on wise living. In simple, straightforward prose, Alan Fox illuminates insights that are often in plain sight but frequently overlooked. A very helpful book."
—**Joseph Goldstein**
Author and co-founder of Insight Meditation Center

"Reading *People Tools* is like having a wise, loving and funny friend take you by the hand, and gently but surely lead you to a better place. Everyone could benefit from reading it."
—**Sharon Salzberg**
Author of *Lovingkindness* and *Real Happiness*

People
Tools
for Business

People
Tools
for Business

50 **STRATEGIES**

*for Building Success,
Creating Wealth, and
Finding Happiness*

ALAN C. FOX

SelectBooks, Inc.
New York

People Tools™ is a trademark of People Tools 13 LLC.

This edition published by SelectBooks, Inc.
For information address SelectBooks, Inc., New York, New York.

First Edition

ISBN 978-1-59079-287-2

Library of Congress Cataloging-in-Publication Data
Fox, Alan C.
People tools for business : 50 strategies for building success, creating wealth, and finding happiness / Alan C. Fox.
pages cm
Summary: "Author of People Tools follows up his first book describing simple strategies for success in our daily lives with more advice that focuses on achieving success in business"-- Provided by publisher.
ISBN 978-1-59079-287-2 (pbk. book : alk. paper) 1. Success in business. 2. Success. I. Title.
HF5386.F524 2014
650.1--dc23
2014018644

Interior book design and production by Janice Benight

Manufactured in the United States of America
10 9 8 7 6 5 4 3 2 1

CONTENTS

This book is dedicated to my teachers—all of my coworkers, clients, friends, and family whom I have been privileged to work and play with during my lifetime. It is also dedicated to you, the reader, the only one who can truly bring these words to life.

In April 2008 my father returned from a tropical vacation far from relaxed. "Sell all your securities," he said. "Now."

He'd spent much of the trip catching up on financial news touting derivatives. But rather than assume the exponential growth in that market signaled an economic boon, Dad saw only the exponential risk of some $500 trillion in promises that banks and insurers didn't have the reserves to keep.

"It's going to be a global crisis, and soon. The worst in our lifetimes."

My broker balked at the order to sell—the market had never been stronger. He enlisted two analysts, who tried valiantly to dissuade me. It didn't work—I sold, and a few months later breathed an enormous sigh of relief to have benefitted, once again, from Dad's unconventional wisdom.

Is it surprising that Alan Fox, an accountant and lawyer by training, a real estate developer by trade, a poet and counselor by fate, would predict a financial meltdown most Wall Street pundits missed? Not if you grew up with him.

Dad anticipated the September 2008 financial crisis because he used an approach that has been a familiar part of his business toolkit for as long as I can remember. Being a Contrarian to him means you question your direction, especially when everyone else seems to be floating with the current. There may be wisdom in crowds, but it takes time to redirect them. So remember to look around and consider another way. An over-leveraged investment, or one not backed by reserves, isn't a long-term solution; it's like a plane that's still flying without enough fuel to reach its destination. And when the house is betting against itself, as banks were betting against their own worthless securities, something is definitely wrong.

Thinking contrary to the flow of popular opinion ("Be a Contrarian"), avoiding a short-term solution to a long-term problem ("Solve It Forward"), letting go of anger ("Ask for a Pineapple Fluff"), and other People Tools have been the cornerstones of my father's success in real estate, business, and life.

These tools, culled over a lifetime of business experience, also helped forge my own career path in real estate law. Starting when I was ten years old, Dad put me to work in his accounting department. After school I trudged to his office and sorted piles of cancelled checks that seemed to multiply each week like brooms in *The Sorcerer's Apprentice*. Important work, he explained. Reviewing his business expenses helped him plan ("Budget, Don't Fudge It"). Comparing expense to income showed him how well his business was doing. And, of course, balancing his business account helped make sure he didn't run out of cash to pay his employees (like me!).

That experience took me three steps up the "Glass Staircase" (confidence, home, experience) before I even knew there was a glass ceiling. At Dad's office I felt both valued and at home, and I gained financial experience that was rare among ten-year-old girls. I confess that at the time this was not exactly the envy of my peers. But now, nearly forty years later, the value—and void—of business mentorship has become an ongoing national debate. Business leaders, social scientists, and management experts have turned their attention to this vital and sometimes elusive component of success, from Daniel Goleman's findings* on the critical role of business mentors in fostering socially intelligent leaders to Sheryl Sandberg's frustrated observation in *Lean In: Women, Work and the Will to Lead* that "searching for a mentor has become the professional equivalent of waiting for Prince Charming."

Wait no more. While the debate rages, read this book—it's like having a long, satisfying conversation with your own professional mentor (and mine), Alan Fox. *People Tools for Business* is rich with

---

* See *Working with Emotional Intelligence*, and "Social Intelligence and the Biology of Leadership," by Daniel Coleman with Richard Boyatzis, *Harvard Business Review*, September 2008.

practical insights and techniques you can use right away, at work and in your life.

As a trial attorney, I use a people toolkit packed with Dad's business insights every day. Flame-mail destroy your morning? "Wait Three Days"—or three hours, and ignore the invective when you respond. Puzzled by a counterproductive position? Look for the "Hidden Agenda." Settlement negotiations? Try to hit all of your client's goals in one shot ("Multi-goaling"). Issuing an ultimatum? Good luck. And be prepared to face the ultimate "audience of one."

My clients have benefitted from many of the tools in this book, which have helped overcome an impasse in negotiations or chart a new, winning litigation strategy. We often start with lemons, and when we do I begin with the tool, "Make Lemonade." You can read more about this approach in the first *People Tools* book, which explains how, when confronted with bad news, you might find a silver lining, or even a pot of gold if you look for it.

Dad gave me a play-by-play of this tool years ago, when the sale of my house fell through two days before escrow was supposed to close. I was furious, and expected to keep the reneging buyer's deposit to cover costs while I relisted the property. Dad advised otherwise.

"But I'm entitled to the *whole* deposit," I protested.

"Offer to keep less, so they have an incentive not to fight about it. And rent for a while. The deposit should help cover your carrying costs, and in six months the market will go up."

By now, you probably can guess he was right. And that I made more money from the eventual sale than if the first deal had closed as planned. If you skip ahead to find the tools of "Life Is an Improv," "Don't Sue the Bastard," and "Delayed Gratification," you'll know why. The buyers were grateful to release only half the deposit, the house rented for more than my monthly carrying costs, and six months later, the market had indeed gone up, so the house sold at higher price that made up for the compromised deposit more than three times over.

The most intractable lawsuit of my career offered a similar "lemonade" type resolution that would have profited everyone involved, much more so than the original real estate deal that had gone awry. Yet litigation raged on for years. The emotional reasons to settle were as good, if not better than the intellectual ones. But somewhere along the way, emotion and intellect had parted ways.

Sometimes "Emotion Trumps Intellect" or vice versa, and perhaps it should. You can read this tool and decide. As in any healthy business relationship, one can have veto power, but the two must work hand in hand. When parties are locked into an emotional agenda untempered by reason, or into an intellectual ultimatum unchecked by emotional reality, there isn't room to "Solve It Forward." It's the litigation cliché described in *A Civil Action*, "whoever comes to their senses first loses"— and so does whoever is the second to come to their senses.

Aha, you say. Isn't there a People Tool for *that*? Well in my business, the right solution at the wrong time is the wrong solution. To discover the right tool, you'll have to "Stick It Out."

You don't have to be a business professional to use *People Tools for Business*. Anyone can use the tools to live a more productive, rewarding life. We're all in the business of achieving goals, large and small. Raising children, keeping house, entertaining friends, or volunteering in our community all involve negotiation and planning. And almost everyone has at least a few business interactions every week. Most of us negotiate a lease or a home purchase at some point. Hiring an accountant, housekeeper, hairdresser, plumber, or neighborhood kid to mow the lawn, bargaining at a garage sale or online auction, and maintaining the household budget are all common business transactions that can benefit from the practical acumen in this book.

Business is built on relationships. Anyone can use the tools in this book to improve that foundation. And when you do, remember to give yourself "Applause."

JILL E. FOX
June 2014
Palo Alto, California

INTRODUCTION

This book is designed to be helpful to everyone who is engaged in the business of life, whether as a student, entrepreneur, worker, or retiree.

We only have today. It's up to each of us to make the most of it.

People
Tools
for Business

TIN WOODMAN

I'll tell you how the Sun rose,—
A Ribbon at a time.
—EMILY DICKINSON
No. 318

The lyf so short, the craft so long to lerne,
Th' assay so hard, so sharp the conquerynge.
—GEOFFREY CHAUCER
The Parliament of Fowls

This book is about business. It's also about the business of life. You are the sole proprietor of your own life. Even if you think you are far from the madding crowd, running your life is very much like running a business, and this book is full of ideas and stories from my own life to help you do exactly that—to run your life well.

When I was very young I knew that I was supposed to be a writer. I'm now seventy-four, and I have taken a long detour through the Oz-like land of commerce. I have followed the yellow brick road to riches. I have met many witches, both evil and good. I have, at times, been Wizard, Scarecrow, and Cowardly Lion. I began with the innocence of Dorothy, and hope I have become like the Tin Woodman and finally earned my heart.

As Geoffrey Chaucer observed more than six hundred years ago, the craft of life takes long to learn. As Emily Dickinson added, more than four hundred years later, each day our life is lit, a little at a time.

1

At work, at home, or in the company of friends, we may use different costumes, but our essential qualities endure.

You can be an employee with predictable hours and a reliable paycheck. You can be an entrepreneur, leaping tall buildings, or falling off a cliff, at a single bound. Or you can be both employee and entrepreneur, either serially or simultaneously. You may be retired and living on a limited income. To discover what you really are at any given moment, observe your "Belt Buckle" (tool #6 in *People Tools*) that reveals where you go and what you really do, not just what you say. And be open to what it is you may become. The essential aspects of your nature will emerge, both sooner and later.

I began my business life as a math tutor one evening when my high school debating partner had something better to do and asked me to take his place. I loved the money, twice the minimum wage at the time, and came to love the teaching.

Even then I realized there are three concentric circles of helping others. First, your family and friends. You see each other often and influence each other greatly. Second, those you mentor. You see each other less frequently and for shorter periods of time (until you become friends). Your influence on each other is less, but still considerable. Third, those who know you through your writing. Your influence as a writer may be diluted by time and distance, but it is focused and circulated more widely, potentially for many years. Ever since I was fifteen years old, in my business and my life, I have been a teacher.

I was delighted when Rina, now almost sixty, introduced herself at the end of a recent reading event at a local bookstore for my first *People Tools* book.

"Remember me? I was your legal secretary when I was nineteen years old."

I did. I recognized her smile.

"I remember," she said, "that whenever I came in late you would tap your watch and say, 'You're one minute late,' or 'You're two minutes late.'"

"I did?"

"Yes. But you also complimented me when I was on time."

"Thank goodness. I hope I've learned a thing or two since then. I wouldn't criticize you today for being late."

"Today I would be on time. I was nineteen then. You taught me a lot. I didn't appreciate most of it until I was older."

We chatted. I reflected on what Rina had just taught me, that she and I are both very different people from who we were forty years ago.

She and her husband bought a book and left.

Today in my life I seldom feel the need to tap my watch or to blame. I don't criticize people for being late. I just recognize that we each have difficulties and differences. I now feel more compassion, including compassion for myself. The tool of Tin Woodman, and this entire book, is about effective compassion.

You may be an employee, entrepreneur, or neither, or both. My goal in *People Tools for Business* is to help you safely and successfully maneuver through the challenges of commerce, which are inseparable from life, using all of your ability to climb as far as you possibly can.

TAKE THE GLASS STAIRCASE

Who knows what women can be when they are finally free to become themselves? Who knows what women's intelligence will contribute when it can be nourished without denying love?... The time is at hand when the voices of the feminine mystique can no longer drown out the inner voice that is driving women on to become complete.

—BETTY NAOMI FRIEDAN
The Feminine Mystique

I'll make him an offer he can't refuse.

—MARIO PUZO
The Godfather

A "glass ceiling" is a political term used to describe "the unseen, yet unbreachable barrier that keeps minorities and women from rising to the upper rungs of the corporate ladder, regardless of their qualifications or achievements."[*]

It is clear that the glass ceiling has been cracked. On January 15, 2014, Mary Barra became the Chief Executive Officer of General Motors. She is the first female CEO of a major global automaker. As of June 2014 there were twenty-four female CEOs of Fortune 500 companies (so they hold the top job at about 4.5 percent of these companies). This is definitely a crack, but by no means a complete breakthrough. There is a lot further to go.

---

[*] Federal Glass Ceiling Commission, 1995.

I say let's remain aware of the glass ceiling, but also start thinking about the Glass Staircase, those translucent steps which everyone, male or female, can climb, depending upon their ability, to reach the upper levels of the corporate hierarchy.

First, I'm going to make an offer of advice which the owner of any business can't refuse: If you fail to hire and promote based first and foremost upon ability, you're going to lose both market share and profit to your competitors who do. Competition today is fierce and global. You're going to need all the best help you can get.

Second, there are five stairs to the top. Using your own ability, these clear steps can be the footing to reach whatever level your skill and determination will allow. To help, you might memorize the acronym CHEAP for the five steps.

1. Confidence
2. Home
3. Education
4. Assertiveness
5. Passion

Confidence. This is the first step on the stairway to success. With confidence you can accomplish just about anything. In his second tenure at Apple, Steve Jobs brought his company from near bankruptcy to the most valuable corporation in the world. Talk about confidence. But in taking that first step you face a chicken-and-the-egg challenge. How can you have authentic confidence before you have achieved success? And how can you achieve success without possessing confidence?

I have two solutions to this dilemma.

First, find a way to build some success, in whatever arena you can find. Join the Toastmasters Club to practice public speaking in a supportive environment. Take dance lessons. Play softball. My ninety-nine-year-old father is the champion of his lawn bowling club and recently was honored by Bowls USA as a member in the elite "Super Shots Club."

Second, act "as if." Remember those lines from *The King and I*, "Whenever I feel afraid, I hold my head erect, and whistle a happy tune, so no one will suspect . . . I'm afraid."

Early in my career in commercial real estate syndication, one of the final questions a potential investor would often ask was, "How well will this investment perform over the next five years?"

The first time I heard this question I was puzzled. I'm human, and it is not given to humans to know what will happen over the next five minutes, let alone the next five years. I was tempted to say, "How the heck should I know?" But that wouldn't instill confidence. What I did say was this:

"None of us can tell what is going to happen over the next five years. But compared with other similar investments available today, this one should do well."

When I gave this answer I usually made the sale.

If you are interviewing for a job, or trying to close a sale, follow the advice of Laszlo Bock who is in charge of all hiring at Google. Show your potential employer or customer the value you offer. And when you do that, by all means exude confidence. Few people ever landed a date by starting with, "I don't suppose you'd like to go out with me."

A few years ago I purchased a shopping center in the Midwest. It had been developed by Howard, a man who had built more than fifty Walmart stores over many years. Walmart is known to be a tough negotiator, so I asked Howard how he persuaded Walmart to hire him in the first place.

"Good question," he said. "Many years ago I found two sites which I thought would appeal to Walmart. I tied both of them up with options and pestered the head of real estate for Walmart until he came out to take a look. He liked both locations and offered to buy them from me at a one million dollar profit.

"I told him that I wanted to build the stores and lease them to Walmart, not just sell the land at a profit. But the Walmart guy balked.

"'You have no experience,' he said. 'We rely on contractors who have already brought in projects on time and at or under budget.'

"I said, 'Tell you what. Let me build the first location for you. If I'm not on time and at or under budget you can buy both sites from me at my cost, and you'll save one million dollars.'

"The Walmart representative agreed. 'Okay,' he said. 'You've got a deal.'"

Howard had firmly placed his foot on the first step of the Glass Staircase: confidence. The other steps, that notably include passion, took him to the very top.

Home. This is the second step on the stairway to success. In your daily life you may have two psychological homes. One is the physical space where you live. The other is the environment where you work.

As much as possible, your physical home must be an oasis of tranquility and support. My favorite part of any vacation is when I return home and walk into my bedroom.

Your "home" at work must also be supportive.

I recently met Janet, who is changing her career. She quit her previous job because she found herself going to bed later and later each night since she knew that when she woke up she was going to have to leave for a job she hated. That's why I recommend that during a job interview you should always ask your potential future coworkers what it's like to work there. Are they treated fairly and with respect?

If you insist on joining a company that is negative toward its employees, or has never promoted a woman past Assistant Director of Human Resources, be my guest. Be a pioneer. But you'll likely end up as the individual with arrows in your back. Better to find a company where the other women feel at home. Maybe a woman even owns the place.

Education. This is the third step. I'm not necessarily talking about a college degree. Google is reported to be "increasingly ready to hire people with no college degrees."[*] But you need to bring value and knowledge and know-how.

---

[*] Tom Friedman. "How to Get a Job at Google, Part 2," *The New York Times*, April, 19, 2014.

When Abraham Lincoln decided to become a lawyer he taught himself law by reading every law book he could get his hands on. Lincoln said about his learning style, "I studied with nobody."

Study with nobody, study with somebody, or study with everybody, but follow your curiosity to learn as much as you possibly can.

As often as possible, I read all the articles of interest to me from the "Most Emailed" section in the *New York Times*. There are many outstanding free courses available on the Internet. I've learned a lot by viewing TED Talks. If you have access to a computer there is no reason today why you can't be well educated. There are so many opportunities to increase your knowledge and value.

Assertiveness. This is the fourth step. As American legend has it, following the custom at the time, Captain Miles Standish asked his friend John Alden to visit Mr. William Mullins and ask for his daughter Priscilla's hand in marriage. Mr. Mullins was agreeable to the idea, and immediately summoned Priscilla. She is renowned for responding, "Prithee, John, why do you not speak for yourself?" As Priscilla and John's great-great-grandson, Rev. Timothy Alden, put it in his *Collection of American Epitaphs and Inscriptions* in 1814, John "soon renewed his visit, and it was not long before their nuptials were celebrated in ample form." Speak for yourself, indeed.

The three A's of Assertiveness are *Ask* (for yourself, Miles Standish), be *Authentic* when you do, and make yourself as *Attractive* as you can.

I recently rented a booth at the Los Angeles Book Festival in order to expand public awareness of my book *People Tools* and also to sell a few copies. Shortly after 9:00 a.m. on an overcast Saturday morning, potential customers began to materialize. I am an inexperienced retailer and was fearful of meeting strangers. I sat toward the back of the booth trying to appear as inconspicuous as I could.

"Alan, you're going to have to talk to people," my marketing coordinator Kat said. "You're the author. They want to hear about the book from you."

"I know. Give me some time."

Ten minutes later my wife approached me. "Alan, Kat has asked me to get you behind the counter. You have to talk to people." I smiled bleakly, and wondered what had possessed me to rent the booth in the first place.

I asked Sean, the experienced proprietor of Gatsby's Books in Long Beach, to help out. Seeing my hesitation, he leaped behind the counter and began to sell my "outstanding" book.

Close to noon I "whistled a happy tune" silently, and began talking to my first potential customer. As the day warmed up, so did I. By Sunday morning I was actually offering my hand and introducing myself. "Hi, I'm Alan. I'm the author." Finally, I even started asking for the sale, and I was rewarded accordingly. I sold seven or eight books, which otherwise we would have had to carry back to my car at the end of the day.

One of Sean's best selling points for my book was his enthusiastic endorsement, which was authentic. Thirty-six years ago I was authentic, by necessity, in persuading my wife to go on our first date. (See "Ticker Tape," another tool in this book.) And yes, I did speak for myself.

And as for Attractiveness, few of us have movie star looks—even movie stars. I once met a former Miss America, who was quite appealing. But she told me she had to spend ninety minutes in front of her mirror each morning fixing her face and hair. That's three hundred ninety hours a year, or almost ten full workweeks. You don't have to be handsome or beautiful to successfully scale the Glass Staircase. And you certainly don't have to spend an hour and a half each day. But you do have to make an effort to present your best natural appearance.

Passion. The fifth and final step to success. As Georg Wilhelm Friedrich Hegel wrote, "We may affirm absolutely that nothing great in the world has been accomplished without passion."[*] And Ludwig van Beethoven said, "I want to seize fate by the throat."[†] Find your

---

[*] George Wilhelm Friedrich Hegel. *The Philosophy of History*, 1932.

[†] Letter to Dr. Franz Wegeler, 1801

passion, seize it, and follow it. My passion is to learn and to help others in any way I can.

The Glass Staircase beckons and is available to all—men, women, children, minorities, majorities—absolutely everyone. If you wish to make the climb, the Glass Staircase is challenging, but it is not too long or too steep for you to complete. But it is up to you to ascend all five stairs:

Confidence
Home
Education
Assertiveness
Passion

Put these all together and success will be yours. And it's CHEAP.

ADVERTISE YOUR MISTAKES

*The great tragedy of Science—the slaying of a
beautiful hypothesis by an ugly fact.*
—THOMAS HENRY HUXLEY
Biogenesis and Abiogenesis

*Look into any man's heart you please, and you will always find, in
every one, at least one black spot which he has to keep concealed.*
—HENRIK IBSEN
Pillars of Society

In a popular TED Talk about vulnerability, University of Houston
social scientist Brene Brown concludes that to attain love and connection you have to let yourself be seen. Deep love and deep connection require authenticity, she says, and there is no way around
that. Darn. And double darn. One of my sons has often said, I hope
humorously, that when you learn to fake sincerity you have it made.

I find that letting myself be seen is scary, which is why I used
to hide behind a façade of flawlessness. This was one of the more
costly mistakes I made in both my business and personal life—the
instances of my absolute refusal to admit that I had made a mistake.
Not a single mistake. Not ever.

When I started out as an attorney more than forty years ago, I
was convinced that I was perfect. Perfect, that is, if you don't count

the two estates I was hired to represent, and which clients later took away from me because I hadn't filed for probate in more than six months. Perfect if you don't count the persistent calls from my client Arnold Gregory, calls which I avoided for a week because I hadn't started to work on his case. Arnold finally wrote to me, "Alan, why are you avoiding me? I just want to send you another client."

I still keep in touch with Jan, one of my first legal secretaries, but I don't ask her what she thought of me then. At that time I was clear that every single mistake made in my office was that of either my law partner or one of our legal secretaries, including Jan. Wouldn't you find this, at best, irritating? I would.

After three or four years of practicing law, and I do mean "practicing," I enrolled in the Counselor Education program at the University of Southern California. I knew very little about either education or counseling, so I could not pretend to be perfect because in that field I didn't even know what perfect was.

And before I learned enough to become dangerous, I realized that other students in the program did not run from me, screaming in the night, if I didn't have the correct answer to every question. They even smiled and offered to help me when I was stuck. And they were not mean or insulting when they "caught" me being ignorant. Sometimes, when I was just plain wrong, my fellow students and professors were understanding and supportive. Maybe they were even secretly pleased that they could help me.

As an experiment I decided to transfer what I had learned in the counseling program to the way I acted at my law firm. I resolved to admit my next mistake to everyone who worked with me. And I did.

Their initial reaction was disbelief. They knew I had made a mistake. They just didn't believe I could be so honest about it. And even as I write this paragraph there's a part of me that still believes that the word "admit" implies weakness. I was afraid that they would be unwilling to follow a leader who made a mistake, especially one who was fragile enough to acknowledge it.

But, to my amazement, their next reaction was relief and reassurance. "We're so glad you told us. We were afraid to point it out to you. What can we do to help?" Incredible! They were trying to help me when I thought they would reject me and begin looking for other jobs.

Their third reaction was to share their own mistakes with me. As a result we all felt closer. It was the first time I really knew what was going on in my own office and with the people who worked there.

Today I tell my staff, "We all make mistakes. Let's hold them to a minimum and learn from them. You make the little mistakes like posting a $200 check to the wrong account or failing to pay a water bill on time. I'll make the big mistakes, like buying a property that loses millions of dollars." And they do. And I have.

My business and personal relationships are far better when I am authentic and willing to confess my mistakes. And because I don't have to hide my blunders, I experience a tremendous sense of relief.

A riddle: When is a mistake not a mistake?

Answer: A mistake is always a mistake, just like a bee sting is always a bee sting. But when you join the flawed human race and admit or even advertise your own imperfections, you will erase the distance between you and your coworkers and between you and your spouse or friends, and you will learn and grow from the experience. Even your boss might be encouraged by your example to recognize that he or she is less than perfect. I said "might be." No boss is perfect.

Admit your mistakes. We each learn more from a mistake, even a big one, than from a triumph. I know that I do.

APPLAUSE

The applause of a single human being is of great consequence.
—SAMUEL JOHNSON
Fables

Where none admire, 'tis useless to excel,
Where none are beaux, 'tis vain to be a belle.
—GEORGE, LORD LYTTELTON
Soliloquy on a Beauty in the Country

Your lifetime is the sum of its parts, and its parts include the other people who move in and out of your life.

In the discussion about the previous tool I recommended that you loudly admit your mistakes. Now I propose that you publically praise others for their triumphs, both honestly and often. You will add luster to their lives, and you will motivate them to excel.

Toward the end of my first year in law school my contracts professor, Richard Wicks, called me into his office.

"Alan, you have a lot of talent. But you aren't applying yourself."

I took this as a huge compliment, partly because I agreed with both statements, but also because I was starved for approval. That he took the time to encourage me was like a double round of applause.

When I was growing up, compliments were rare. My father believed that admiration smothers ambition. So while he bragged about me to his friends, he seldom, if ever, praised me to my face. "Why the B+?"

was his comment about my report cards on each of the few times I earned less than an A. It's a small wonder I found it difficult to offer to others the standing ovation I myself had never received. Unfortunately, words of admiration still spring slowly from my lips.

I say "unfortunately" because I think that my business, and my life, would improve if I consistently applied applause more liberally.

I was an unknown author when *People Tools* was published in January 2014. Jane Wesman, my publicist, worked very hard to line up a number of interviews for me—radio interviews which I dreaded. I always want to succeed on the highest level, but on these interviews I was starting from scratch, as I had little previous experience with the media. Fortunately, my second appearance was an hour-long interview on *The Self Improvement Show* with Irene Conlan who was very complimentary about my book. She compared *People Tools* to a self-help book published in 1986, which has sold more than 6,000,000 copies. She predicted my book would be a best seller. That did a lot for my confidence. Today, with more confidence and more practice, I almost enjoy radio interviews. I say "almost," because I'm still not entirely comfortable putting myself out there in public before thousands of people.

Though I worry that might sound immodest (I hope that my work will speak, or whisper, for itself), I do strongly believe in sharing my process so that you will know that I, too, struggle with a number of self-confidence issues. Don't we all? I read once that an English stage actor of great renown actually is nervous to the point of physical illness before each of his performances.

So I always try to make an effort to acknowledge the other people in my life. During radio interviews, when it is true, I often say "good question" before I answer. I am always enthusiastic when one of my children or grandchildren reports a success. Last weekend my granddaughter Claire performed in her college concert choir, in which membership is quite an honor. My wife and I flew to Oregon to be in the audience. Just making the trip is one form of applause. We were delighted to offer her formal applause too at the end of the performance.

But formality can also keep us at a distance. I address people by their first name. Being present and unpretentious allows us to appreciate each other close up.

At a formal dinner a few years ago I asked one of President Obama's assistants if I could use the president's first name to greet him. "Nooooo. Call him 'Mr. President.'" When he appeared, I forgot.

"Hi, Barack," I said. I quickly caught my mistake. "I mean, Mr. President."

He smiled. "Barack is okay." He put me at ease.

The most successful National Basketball Association coach in history, Phil Jackson, tells us in his outstanding book *Sacred Hoops* that he values the superstars such as Michael Jordon or Kobe Bryant not so much for their own performance and statistics, but for how much they help to improve the play of their teammates.

Your life and your business are team sports. "Good work!" Do you like to hear that? So do your employees, your boss, your friends, your children and, Heavens to Betsy, even your partner or spouse.

With deference to Benjamin Franklin, I suggest that God best helps those who help each other—not just themselves.

Lady Gaga sings, "I live for the applause, applause, applause."

We all do. So let's start clapping!

LEAVE GRUMPY AT HOME

Paradise is where I am.
—VOLTAIRE
Le Mondain

By happy alchemy of mind,
They turn to pleasure all they find.
—MATTHEW GREEN
The Spleen

I opened my law office in 1968. At that time my first wife and I had been married about seven years. We had enjoyed each other's company almost every minute of that time, but then we began to argue.

I don't think the arguments had anything to do with my starting a law practice (though it's impossible to know for sure). What I do know is that our disagreements often began before I left for work in the morning. So by the time I reached my office, and even before facing the new challenges that the day would bring, I was already upset. I would throw open the front door, scowl at our receptionist, and stride nonstop to my corner office.

After more than six months of, from time to time, openly displaying my unhappiness, I noticed that productivity in my office had begun to resemble the daily fluctuations of the stock market. In my office the lows were not caused by economic news or greed or fear, but rather by a single variable—me.

When I walked in angry, everyone talked about what was going on with me for an hour or two before they started any real work.

"Alan is upset today. Stay out of his way."

"Don't do your salary review today. He's awfully stingy when he's fighting with his wife."

If I cared about anything at work, I cared about efficiency. I wanted maximum productivity for each paycheck I signed. So I decided to revise my attitude. (All too often I find that I do the right thing for the wrong reason.)

Each morning when I stepped out of my car in the parking lot I put on a smile. I thought about something pleasant as I rode the elevator up to the eighth floor. I greeted my employees with a friendly, "Good morning. Glad to see you."

The productivity of my staff immediately improved. I was surprised that my own productivity also improved. Dramatically. I didn't waste an hour or two in the morning continuing an unproductive argument in my head. Some days I even forgot about an ongoing disagreement. My mind became more clear when I focused on business rather than on outside grievances.

Skip to the present. Several weeks ago I was late for my yoga lesson. I am often late, probably because I prefer forty-five minutes of yoga rather than the seventy-five minutes I signed up for. This time my yoga teacher seemed grumpy with me for being tardy.

"Ellen," I said. "You provide a service, which is to share with me a pleasant lesson. I realize that if I worked hard for the full seventy-five minutes I might learn more and feel better. But if the experience isn't pleasant I will probably quit, and lose all the benefit. I'm happy to pay for all of your time, even when I'm late, and I think we'll both enjoy the experience more if we greet each other with a smile."

Ellen smiled. I was glad I said something. Now I arrive on time and don't miss a minute. I even look forward to lessons. And current scientific research indicates that the very act of smiling will improve your mood.

Every week I work at least fifty hours. That's about 45 percent of the approximately one hundred twelve hours I'm awake. If I didn't enjoy this time, which is almost half of my waking hours, I wouldn't have much of a life.

So when you're at work or any place that requires interaction with other people, leave Grumpy at home where he belongs. If your boss is Grumpy, treat him or her to a smile and a copy of this book. If Grumpy is in your mind, sneak Happy into your head instead. Life is much too short to spend with Grumpy as a permanent guest.

DON'T RUN OUT OF CASH

From birth to age eighteen, a girl needs good parents. From eighteen to thirty-five, she needs good looks. From thirty-five to fifty-five, she needs a good personality. From fifty-five on, she needs good cash.

—SOPHIE TUCKER
Said at age sixty-nine

In our wholly factitious society, to have no cash at all means frightful want or absolute powerlessness.

—GEORGE SAND
Histoire de Ma Vie

My wife Daveen has been known to visit McDonald's with two dollars in her purse. Once she bought five dollars' worth of food and promised to bring back the additional three dollars in a few hours. They gave her the food.

Hey, Daveen, it's McDonald's. This is a huge corporation with a zillion franchisees. This is not your local family pharmacy that might stake you to a few bucks. I wouldn't have the nerve to ask McDonald's to loan me money.

Don't run out of cash.

When I started out in real estate I would find a property, open escrow with a small deposit, and promise to pay the down payment in sixty or ninety days. In those days I always tried to have three potential sources of funds available to me to close escrow. None of them was my own bank account, because I seldom had enough money in the bank.

First, I turned to my father. I always appreciated the fact that my dad would gladly loan me money, and that he'd only charge the interest rate he was earning at the bank.

I remember the time when my real estate partner Harvey met my dad at his bank to pick up a $6,000 cashier's check we needed to close an escrow. Before handing over the check, my dad insisted that Harvey sign for it.

My second source was to sell the property to investors and collect their money before I had to pay to the escrow company. This was more than a little iffy. I usually found investors within sixty days after close, but not before.

The third source was a bank loan. Sometimes this source was available, sometimes not. I still remember being turned down by my local bank because they didn't think I could repay the $35,000 I requested. Twelve years later I was swarmed upon by at least seven solicitous employees of the same bank when I converted an $8,000,000 cashier's check from an escrow company into three different cashier's checks, each destined for another bank. As the saying goes, living well is the best revenge.

After two or three years in the business, my need for funds sometimes rose to more than $100,000 and my lender of first resort, my dad, was not able to cover such a large amount. I had to arrange for a bank line of credit in advance.

Years ago I read an article in the *Wall Street Journal,* in which the author said that he did not like business professors, but did like a one-day workshop he attended given by a professor from Harvard Business School who presented his ten rules of business:

Rule Number One: Don't run out of cash.

Rule Number Ten: Don't run out of cash.

The other eight rules, the professor said, were not nearly as important.

In my current business, I've made sure to never end up in a situation where I don't have enough cash to pay my employees. As a result, I earn my employees trust. I know this because they show up five days a week, smile at me, and do what I ask them to do. Many have been with me for more than twenty years. I have found enough money to meet my payroll every two weeks for the past forty-five years. That's more than 1,170 payrolls.

The story is told of the ninety-four-year-old Texas billionaire who married a twenty-five-year-old former Miss America. After several years of marriage he asked his lovely wife, "Darling, if I lost all of my money would you still love me?"

"Honey, of course I would still love you. I would miss you, but I would love you."

I don't want my employees to miss me. I don't want my lenders to miss me and charge huge default interest payments while they do. I don't want my landlord to miss me after throwing me out of my offices.

The best way to avoid running out of cash is to predict your cash flows accurately and conservatively in advance. That's why I keep two budgets at all times. One is for large cash items such as closing an escrow and receiving money from my investors. The second budget is for my regular monthly income and expenses.

Since real estate is inherently cyclical—that means money in and money out is inherently unpredictable—I paid off the loan on my home as soon as I could. And I will never take out another loan on my home, no matter how tempting that may be. Today's interest rates on home loans are attractive, but I want to sleep soundly every night, without fear of ever being forced out of my home.

One of my acquaintances in real estate earned more than $7,000,000 in the prosperous years of 2002 through 2007. Then the commercial real estate market collapsed, and with it his entire net worth—from a high of $20,000,000 to minus $4,000,000. That's right—he lost more than everything he had in only two years. Last week he spent a full day in a Seattle courtroom with his attorney attempting to settle a $50,000 loan, which he still owed and could not readily pay. And this loan is one of many that still prevent him from sleeping soundly.

For your own sake, whether in business or your personal life, predict your cash flow as accurately as you can—every day or every week, if necessary. Be conservative, not optimistic.

And DON'T RUN OUT OF CASH.

THE (DREADED)
ANNUAL REVIEW

*Prayer indeed is good, but while calling on the gods
a man should himself lend a hand.*
—HIPPOCRATES
Regimen

*With affection beaming in one eye,
and calculation shining out of the other.*
—CHARLES DICKENS
Martin Chuzzlewit

"How much is my annual raise?" This is the question on everyone's mind when supervisor and employee meet for the (dreaded) annual review.

Whose review? The employee's, of course. How did the employee perform during the past twelve months, as measured by a (subjective) supervisor applying the employer's criteria? Productivity, attitude, and attendance all figure into the beady-eyed calculation.

If I asked a hundred managers, "What is your goal in conducting an annual review?" most would answer, "To give the employee information on job performance, such as where he or she failed and what he or she should improve upon next year, and to reveal the amount of next year's compensation."

Years ago I would have agreed, which is why I used to postpone annual employee reviews for three or four months beyond their

29

anniversary date. Why? Because I feared that the review would be unpleasant for me. First, I was going to have to criticize my employees and let them know, for instance, that spending two hours a day on Facebook was unacceptable. Second, I was going to either keep their salary the same, risking their resentment, or give them a raise in pay, thereby shrinking my own bank account.

In the movie *Coconuts* the hotel employees of a mustachioed Groucho Marx chased him from the lobby and up a flight of stairs.

"We want our money," they yelled.

"What do you mean?"

"We want our money," they repeated.

"I don't understand. You want whose money?" Groucho shouted back.

"You haven't paid us. We want to be paid!"

"Oh," says Groucho, pointing directly at them. "**You** want **my** money," with emphasis on the "my."

But I digress, which is not uncommon for me when I am faced with a situation I find uncomfortable.

But let's take the word "Dreaded" out of The Annual Review and look at it bit differently.

First, why should we think of the review as being about the employee? Don't both the employee and employer want the best possible performance? If you are an employee and don't perform as well as you can, perhaps you lack the proper tools or training. Maybe you don't feel appreciated and, as a result, are not as involved as you might be. I regard tools, training, and the expression of appreciation as the responsibility of the employer, not the employee.

Second, why shouldn't I want to encourage the best performance possible and pay fairly for that performance? If all of my forty-five or so employees felt unfairly treated and failed to show up Monday morning, my business would instantly disappear. Each of them is excellent at what they do and could easily find a position somewhere else. But how could I reconstruct, entirely by myself, the outstanding team we have built together over the past forty-five years?

I now regard the annual review as a review of my own performance. I think of my employees as coworkers. We work in the same building, write e-mails to outsiders and to each other, talk on the telephone, and enjoy lunch in early afternoon. Every one of us is a crew member on the same ship, headed in the same direction.

Today my ideal procedure for the annual review is:

1. To keep my coworkers up to date regularly on how they are doing throughout the year. When your flight lands in San Francisco, it's too late to remind yourself that you should have boarded the flight for Chicago. I offer approval to encourage them, though not as often as I should. I suggest course corrections to help them focus on what needs to be changed. In the old days I would say to an employee after his or her first day on the job, "I've decided to renew your option. You can come back tomorrow."

   Today I cringe at the thought of how I would feel if my new boss of one day said that to me. Now I ask a new employee for their input. Two weeks ago I hired Joy to help with the marketing and promotion of *People Tools*. At the end of her first week I asked, "Are all of us providing proper information and support so that you can do your best work?" If you have properly helped your coworkers during the year there will be no bad surprises for either of you at the annual review.

2. When it's time for the annual review, I make sure to conduct it within a week or two of the anniversary date. It's not fair to my coworkers to delay information which is important to them and keep them walking on eggshells, waiting for "the axe to drop." And I don't want to skulk about the office hiding from someone.

3. Ask each person being reviewed to evaluate him or herself and to write down their accomplishments of the past year and goals for the coming year. Not only

does this help your employees learn the valuable skill of self-assessment, it also shows how much you respect and appreciate their opinions.

4. Ask the reviewees what salary they think they deserve. I use their recommendation as a guide. Years ago I had an employee, Gert, who, always asked for a ten or fifteen percent raise, which was far too high. But at least I knew what she was thinking. It gave us the opportunity to discuss her expectations and she worked with me for almost twenty-five years. One year Cathy, my vice president and general manager, asked for a raise that was far too small. I increased her salary by three times the amount she had requested.

5. During the review I ask how I, or other managers, can better assist our coworkers to perform better. "Replace my seven-year-old computer," was one answer. I was embarrassed. I had allowed a valued member of my accounting staff to struggle for two years with entirely outdated equipment. Sometimes you learn about a very inexpensive adjustment that has a huge pay-off in productivity or morale.

6. If a member of your team has made an outstanding contribution to the company that saves time and money, increases profits and productivity, or improves the working conditions in the office, consider awarding a one-time bonus. This way, the annual review can be just as much about rewarding performance as it is about offering constructive suggestions on how to improve.

   Why shouldn't you want to encourage the best performance possible and pay fairly for that performance? If all of your employees felt unfairly compensated and failed to show up for work, your business might immediately vanish. Each of them is there because they are needed, and most could easily find a position somewhere else.

7. If my goal is to retain my team member for another full year, I sometimes pay part of their increased salary as a bonus at their next anniversary date. We all like something "extra," and often a $2,000 bonus looms larger than $166.67 a month before payroll taxes.

8. Be prepared at an annual review to be flexible about hours of work (some people prefer to begin their work day at 6:00 a.m.) and time away from the office for personal matters. One of the biggest perks I enjoy myself, as an entrepreneur and business owner, is that I can set my own hours. I can take off Thursday afternoon and come in on Saturday morning if I like. So I refuse to be a prison warden for my staff. They work with me to accomplish a mission, not to lose their freedom to visit a doctor when they need to, or watch their daughter's soccer finals.

When I improve as a manager, my coworkers improve at their positions. That is why I no longer dread reviewing them, because, in reality, we are helping each other. And I am reviewing myself as much as my coworkers. If I keep up to date and keep the communication flowing during the year, we both can anticipate—rather than dread—the Annual Review.

Let's take "Dreaded" out of The Annual Review.

PEOPLE TOOL 8 FOR BUSINESS

READY, AIM . . .

The one task managers universally dislike is firing an employee, and for good reason: it isn't fun. One time I planned to fire my receptionist on Friday afternoon at three minutes before the end of her workday. Unfortunately, she disappeared five minutes early and I had to fire her by telephone. That was unpleasant, particularly because I had to face her again Monday morning when she returned her keys and picked up her personal items.

Even when I am dissatisfied with an employee I don't like to "fire" him or her. The "Ready, Aim . . . " part is easy, but "Fire!" Ay, there's the rub. Most of us hesitate to pull the trigger because we anticipate that there will be hurt feelings. We risk crying (from them), anger (also theirs, directed at us), or vigorous threats and counterattacks. We might also empathize with a coworker who is going to be out of a job.

I've had to fire many employees over my forty-five years as president of my own company. And while I still have trouble pulling the trigger, I've come to see "firing" people in a new light. Shakespeare wrote in *Hamlet* that "There is nothing good or bad but thinking makes it so." When it comes to letting someone go, I've found that what I might otherwise consider "bad" actually leads to better opportunities for my employee.

And for the health of my organization the "Fire!" is almost always a benefit. I recently fired Alisa and hired Linda, whose work and work ethic are far better than her predecessor's. It was a good choice for my organization. And ultimately it was a good choice for Alisa as well. She was free to find a job she will be better suited for, and in which she could be more appreciated. In fact she did.

Years ago my friend John (who helped me "Climb a Mountain" in chapter 50 of my original *People Tools* book) called me late one morning.

"Today the magazine finally fired me," he said.

"Are you in Los Angeles?"

"Yes."

"I'll join you for dinner."

When I arrived John had already emptied half a bottle of wine.

"Congratulations," I said.

"Huh?"

"Congratulations, John. On losing your job."

"Why 'congratulations'? Now I'm out of work."

"John, you've complained to me about that job for the last ten years. Now you don't have to do it anymore. You're free to pursue other opportunities, to write the novel you've always talked about. In six months you'll be much happier."

John smiled. He didn't quite believe me, but recognized my tendency to look at the bright side of everything. Though John didn't warm up right away to the advantages of his sudden unemployment, we both enjoyed our dinner together and catching up on each other's lives. And as you might have guessed, six months later John was bragging to me about not having enough time to work on all of his exciting new projects.

When I opened my own law firm at age twenty-seven, I was reluctant to fire anyone. It took me six months to finally tell one of my legal secretaries Judy that her work was not up to my standard. She pleaded and cried before she left.

A year and a half later I walked into the lunchroom of the same office building, and there was Judy. When she saw me, she beamed.

"Remember me?" she said.

"Of course I remember you."

"Now I'm working for the attorney in the penthouse." She was definitely rubbing in the fact that my office was only on the 8th floor.

"Congratulations. That's great!" I was relieved. Maybe she hadn't collected too much from my unemployment insurance account.

"And he thinks I'm the best secretary he's ever had." Judy was obviously pleased with herself, and more than happy to share her improved status.

I believed her. I know that my requirements are high and that many capable people fall short. The "attorney in the penthouse" might well find a reject from my law office to be an outstanding contributor in his. Perhaps Judy's new boss was a better manager, or more encouraging, than I was at that time.

Not too long ago Edward, a cousin of mine, was admitted to a prestigious business school. But the school deferred his admission for two years and required Edward to acquire work experience before entering the MBA program. Edward declared that he was very interested in commercial real estate, so I offered him a generous salary to be my intern for two years. Visions of sugarplums danced in my head. Here was a bright young man raising my entire organization to a higher level. I also assumed that anyone who wanted a career in commercial real estate would jump at the chance to learn all about the business from me, and would leave the office reluctantly after a fourteen-hour work day.

Silly me. During his first week on the job Edward asked me if he could take a half hour for lunch (instead of an hour) and then leave half an hour early every day. I was stunned. Early in my own real estate career, a man who had established himself in commercial real estate had agreed to show me the ropes. The only problem was that he arrived at his office at 6:00 p.m. and worked until 4:00 in the morning. I was still practicing law, so after a full day of work I drove to his office to help out, free of charge. I assumed that Edward would be as committed as I had been.

After eight months of clock-watching and limited productivity, I told Edward that his internship wasn't working out, and that he would have to leave at the end of one year rather than two. He immediately began to look for a new position and soon found one.

Six months later I arrived home one evening to find Edward talking to my wife. After all, we did remain cousins.

"Hi, Alan," he said.

"Hi, Edward. How's your new job?"

"Absolutely fantastic. I'm with a company that electronically places products into videos."

"Like visually adding a can of Coke on someone's desk?"

"Exactly." Then Edward went on to describe why he'd been thrilled to work until 3:30 a.m. the previous night to finish a "rush" assignment. He seemed elated to be spending eighty hours a week at his new job, after resenting his forty hours a week with me.

My point is this—it's vital for each of us to find our personal niche in life and then occupy it. For each of us there are jobs, and companies, which work for us as well as we for them. Many people hate working in an office and would prefer to be a waiter or a forest ranger. Some people gravitate toward situations that require them to be away from home for days or weeks at a time. My friend Valerie was a masseuse for many years. Then she became an acupuncturist and was delighted to join the staff of Celebrity Cruises to travel the world for a year. Some people love to maneuver numbers, like I do. Others prefer to interact with people. There is no "good" or "bad" here. There is only personal preference.

Only after John was fired could he find the life he wanted all along.

After I fired Judy she found a niche in which she was a star.

Edward was fully engaged, rather than repelled, by his second internship.

The following quotation is attributed to the humorist Will Rogers.

"Investing in stocks is easy. You buy a stock, it goes up, you sell it. If the stock doesn't go up, don't buy it in the first place."

My first advice to you is that if an employee doesn't work out, don't hire him or her in the first place. But if you do end up with an employee who doesn't work out for you, do not hesitate to call in your human resources department (which might be you) and prepare for "Ready, Aim . . ."

YOU ARE NOT IN THE BUSINESS OF MAKING TELEPHONE CALLS

Let the end try the man.
—SHAKESPEARE
King Henry the Fourth, Part II

'Tis a lesson you should heed,
Try, try again.
If at first you don't succeed,
Try, try again.
—THOMAS H. PALMER
Teacher's Manual

One week on a Friday, my receptionist Barbara got stuck in our elevator that had stopped between floors. The telephone in the elevator didn't work, but fortunately the elevator malfunctioned during normal office hours and Barbara used her cell phone to summon help. We flipped an electric breaker and the elevator began to move.

Obviously, this was a situation which had to be corrected immediately. Others, including me, work on weekends and no one wants to be trapped in an elevator for a few hours, or a few days.

Irene, who is in charge of our building operations, was out of the office but was immediately notified. Five days later no one from the elevator service company had shown up to fix the problem. At 11:40 a.m. on the following Tuesday I received an e-mail from Irene:

"I would like to apologize for not following up with Trifecta Elevator Service on Friday, as they promised me they would be at the office Friday afternoon to ensure the elevator was operating correctly. I was unaware that Trifecta never showed up until yesterday morning. Thank you and rest assured this will not happen again. I will make sure to follow-up with vendors if I am away from the office. Appreciate your understanding."

My first reaction was that her "appreciate your understanding" was premature.

My second reaction was that we are not in the business of making telephone calls or writing e-mails. We are in the business of making things happen—in this case, making sure the unreliable elevator was immediately repaired.

If you are a salesman you are not in the business of making calls, either by telephone or in person. You are in the business of generating sales. You are not evaluated on how many phone calls you make during a day. The only real measurement of your success is how many actual sales you produce.

If you are a manager you are not in the business of telling people to perform tasks. You are in the business of following through to be certain that their assignments have actually been completed on time and to appropriate standards.

If you are a writer, as I am today, you are not in the business of writing 5,000 words. You are in the business of communicating clearly and in an interesting way to your potential readers.

A number of my top people have been with me for many years. They reached their positions and higher compensation, but not by making telephone calls or sending e-mails. They have achieved career success by producing desired results. And none of them are very good at making excuses. They don't have to be.

BUDGET, DON'T FUDGE IT

Never promise more than you can perform.
—PUBLILIUS SYRUS
Maxim 528

We never know how high we are
Till we are called to rise;
And then, if we are true to plan,
Our statures touch the skies.
—EMILY DICKINSON
No. 1176

If you intend to be successful in business, or in life, it helps to have a plan, especially a financial plan. Double entry bookkeeping began in the 13th century and is the gold standard for every modern business. A budget is merely a money blueprint. It will help you run your business and your life more effectively.

The theory of a financial budget is pretty simple. Write down all of the income which you reasonably expect to receive in your next operating period, usually a month or year, and then write down all of the expenses which you reasonably expect to incur. Include enough categories of income and expense to make your budget meaningful. How much do you expect to spend for rent, for transportation, for telephone? Then take your total expected (budgeted) income, subtract your total expected (budgeted) expenses, and violà! You have your budgeted net profit (or loss).

To make a budget, you don't need to be an expert in the finer points of budgeting, like the difference between cash and accrual accounting. These subjects are fully covered in many business texts. I will tell you that if you create a budget that you like, and have been realistic in creating it, you're in business. At the end of your reporting period, usually a calendar year, you're going to be faced with financial statements that tell you how close you actually came to meeting your budget. If you follow my suggestions, the difference between your budget (which was your best guess) and your financial statements (which is what really happened) will be pretty close and you will have few, if any, bad surprises.

In the early 1990s my brother David began his own business. David was a licensed California attorney and served under Governor Jerry Brown as the California Real Estate Commissioner.

But in his own business, David frequently asked for my advice.

"Sure. Let me see your financial statements," I would say.

"I don't have them yet. Maybe in a few weeks."

Like many of us, although he was very successful in other aspects of his life, David had a mental block against numbers. I'm sure he never even considered using a budget. As a result he probably didn't know how well, or poorly, his business was performing until late the following year when he finally filed his income tax returns. But by then it was too late for him to do anything about it.

My first advice is that it's important to get your budget down on paper, no matter how simple you think it is. When my partner and I started our law firm on April 1, 1967, we had a rudimentary budget. This consisted of how much money we had in the bank (very little), and how much income we expected to receive each month, set off against how much our monthly costs might be. Fortunately, we had one client who was paying us a monthly retainer of $3,000 (which is probably the equivalent of $25,000 today) and relatively few expenses, which consisted of $540 a month for rent and $600 a month for our legal secretary's salary, insurance, telephone, and all those other pesky items which have a nasty habit of popping up more often than anyone expects. Our budget was simple, but it existed only in our heads.

A year later I began to buy real estate and budgeting became more important and more complex. I was buying single-family houses and promising to pay a fortune—$2,500—as a down payment for each house. On the very first day of my company, Friday, March 1, 1968, I toured thirteen houses, offered to buy eleven, and ended up with nine. The one small problem was that I didn't have the cash to close escrow. Without a concrete budget, I was unable to accurately predict my cash flow and got myself into a jam. Fortunately, several of my law clients invested in four or five of the houses, and my dad was willing to loan me the rest of the money I needed.

I was lucky, but I realized that I could no longer carry the numbers around solely in my head. I had taken a bookkeeping course in high school, and beginning in 1968 I began to maintain two separate budgets. The first was for my own personal monthly expenses. The second was for high ticket items such as buying houses to rent, where the amounts of money were, for me, quite high and the sources (investors or borrowing from my dad) less certain.

I then updated those budgets once or twice every week for many years. One was for regular items so that I would know that I had enough income to pay recurring monthly personal expenses. The second was for those "big ticket" items—real estate I had agreed to purchase and the projected money I would receive from investors as they "bought in" to each property.

I must confess that when I first started buying and managing single-family houses, and then apartment buildings, I scrupulously maintained financial reports for current operations, but for the first ten years or more I had no operating budgets. None. So how could I compare the actual result with our expected result? I couldn't. I had no budget and I was flying blind. Fortunately, I didn't crash, but I do not recommend taking that chance.

The biggest advantage of using a budget in your personal or business life is that, if you follow it, you will spend less money than you expect to bring in. Let's take dining out as an example. When I am invited to lunch or dinner with a friend I like to say "Yes." If I had a monthly food budget, however, I might say to myself, "I only have $45 left in my food budget for this month, and it has to last until Sunday. Maybe we can have lunch at my house, or a neighborhood café, or wait until next month unless, of course, my friend wants to treat."

The second advantage of a budget in your personal or business life is that, if it is reasonably accurate (though you can't always know for sure in advance), you won't run out of money. Even a bank, which will issue you a credit card and conveniently give you months or years to pay your bill, will eventually insist you pay all of the money back. That's where budgeting is valuable. You won't be seduced by easy credit and find you can't pay your rent at the beginning of next month.

The third advantage of a budget is that you might decide not to enter a losing business in the first place. Ed, a friend of mine, is in the furniture business in Arizona. I have rented retail space to Ed, but he never signs a lease until a realistic budget assures him that his new store will earn a profit. The bad news for me is that Ed drives a very hard bargain. The good news for me is that he always pays his rent on time.

At this point some of you might be feeling like my brother David, saying to yourself, "I don't like the idea of budgeting, I'm afraid of numbers, and I'm not going to do this."

Fair enough. Without a formal budget you can still be highly successful in life and, perhaps, in business. But if you are unable to do it for yourself I respectfully suggest that you hire an accountant to prepare a simple budget for you, and then have your accountant inform you every three or six months about how you are doing. There used to be a TV ad for a large manufacturer's auto service department. A uniformed serviceman says, "You can either pay me now, or you can pay me later."

You can make your own budget or pay an accountant now, or you can pay an attorney a lot more money later when you run into trouble.

When you have a budget, be it in your head or written down, whether it's for money, or how to better allocate your time (most of us keep our appointments on a calendar, which is very similar to a budget), you will have a roadmap to follow to greater success, and I'm confident you will experience less pain and more pleasure in your life.

A budget? You really can't very well fudge it.

MAKE LITTLE DEALS YOUR BIG DEAL

*If you should put even a little on a little, and should
do this often, soon this too will become big.*

—HESIOD
Works and Days

Great deeds are usually wrought at great risks.

—HERODOTUS
The Histories of Herodotus

When I was eighteen I worked as a stock boy in a warehouse
earning minimum wage. It didn't take me long to figure out that my
father took in more money from his two modest real estate investments before I left for work in the morning than I was going to earn
working an entire day in the warehouse. I decided early on that I
didn't want to earn money for the rest of my life by selling my time.
I thought that investments were the better way to go.

Fifty-six years later, I'm happy that I decided to go down that
path, though I know it's not for everyone. Some of us are entrepre-
neurs, and some of us are employees who prefer the security of a
salary. And some of us are both. No problem. It's a matter of taste.

For those who do venture down the path of entrepreneurship,
no matter to what degree, I want to share with you one of the most
important lessons that I was fortunate to learn early on.

When I was young and ambitious I worked for several months on a project that would have taken five years to fully accomplish. A banker, David Maloney, suggested to me over lunch one day that I should shift my focus to smaller deals where I could complete one or two each month, rather than committing to a single venture which would take years to pay off, if it paid off at all. I remember David Maloney's name because his guidance, from more than fifty years ago, was among the best I have ever received.

On his advice, I turned to smaller deals, such as investing in single-family rental homes, then apartments, and finally office buildings and retail shopping centers. These smaller deals have been the bedrock of my financial empire. I have always avoided any single investment, which even if extremely attractive, was so big that if it failed it would sink my business ship. Because then I wouldn't be captain any more. It does happen.

And while my general strategy has been to focus on smaller deals, there have been some costly exceptions.

I once paid more than $100 million for a shopping center with almost half a mile of frontage on Scottsdale Boulevard in Scottsdale, Arizona. I remember flying by private jet to an early morning meeting with the owner, in order to beat the competition. During the "Great Recession" of 2007–2012 this property was foreclosed at a significant loss.

The third largest investment I ever made was the purchase of an outstanding downtown property in Denver, Colorado, for more than $60 million. Unfortunately, the escrow closed on August 22, 2008, a few weeks before September 15, 2008. That was the day Lehmann Brothers filed for bankruptcy and the worldwide financial meltdown began in earnest. Five years later I sold that property at a small loss. As Hesiod observed more than 2,500 years ago, "Observe due measure, for right timing is in all things the most important factor."

Several years ago I purchased eight businesses, including a world famous nightclub, from a multi-billion dollar investment company. That venture ended in the investment company suing me in two states, causing me a great deal of aggravation for more than a year of my life.

For an opening shot the investment company served my then ninety-five-year-old father with a summons and complaint in one of their lawsuits against me, even though their CEO had previously visited me in my office.

The process server knocked; my dad opened the door.

"Mr. Fox?"

"Yes."

"You're served!" And they threw the summons and complaint at him. Because my father was not involved in any way in the lawsuit, I cannot think of any reason they would serve him instead of me, except to try to intimidate.

Fortunately I believe in open communication and had already told my father about the potential litigation. I had no idea that he would be served rather than me. But we shared a good laugh.

Ultimately that deal was a financial mini-disaster. And though we finally settled, I relearned that important lesson David Maloney had taught me many years before: don't let the glamour or size of the deal get in the way of the bottom line. I'd rather invest in something that is boring, small, and profitable than in something big and exciting that will not be a financial success.

As an old saying reminds us, "Tall oaks from little acorns grow."

Leave the big or seemingly exciting deal to others, or to yourself when you can afford to spend years of your precious time on it, and when the outcome will not significantly alter your life. It may be money we're after but, for me, money is only useful in the service of joy.

I know that we all read newspaper stories about high risks which led to high rewards. It does happen, but be careful. Even Warren Buffet has become a big deal by starting with many little deals. He is quoted as sharing the following philosophy: "I don't look to jump over seven-foot bars; I look around for one-foot bars that I can step over." His percentage of success is high, but not his percentage of risk.

Little deals are a big deal.

WAIT THREE DAYS

Are you a gunslinger? Do you answer your e-mails a few minutes before you receive them? Do you stride through the fog of war without a moment's hesitation?

I have an idea. Slow down. Take it easy. Wait Three Days.

I developed this tool several years after I began to practice law. In those ancient times everyone relied on delivery of the mail for communications, which came twice a day. That mail sometimes brought a nasty surprise, such as a notice from the Internal Revenue Service, or yet another legal pleading from a major law firm designed to force me to spend time and my client's money in a war of attrition. Oftentimes these letters would blot out the warmth of any emotional sun which had been shining on my life—letters which, when I read them, destroyed my day.

I gradually realized that, no matter how strong the aggravation, three days later it always blended into the background "noise" of my professional life and didn't bother me any more than my many other business challenges.

One morning I received a letter from one of my former law partners, Jim. Jim had recently moved out of our offices and formed a new law firm, which was, I think, a result of my increased focus on buying, selling, and managing commercial real estate, when he preferred to practice law. A year before he left I told Jim that I was generating three quarters of the total profit from our real estate investments and thought I should receive two thirds of our earnings, rather than the original agreement of a 50-50 split. Jim insisted on receiving his 50 percent from the real estate or, as an alternative, I could invest in real estate by myself and keep 100 percent of what I earned. I chose the second option. When Jim left we agreed that he could take his 50 percent share of the real estate portfolio that we co-owned and which I continued to manage.

Which brings me back to the letter. It arrived months after Jim left. In it, he claimed that I had cheated him. First, he accused me of letting one of his buildings fall into disrepair. Second, we had purchased twenty-seven refrigerators for the same building and only three were left. Clearly, he said, I had stolen twenty-four refrigerators. His letter ended with the threat to sue me for $20,000.

As you can imagine, I was incensed. Fortunately, I followed the advice of Miguel de Cervantes ("Think before thou speakest") and waited three days. Then I called him.

"Hi, Jim."

"Hi."

"I'm calling about your letter which I received earlier this week."

"Yes?"

"In it you claim that I failed to properly maintain your property, stole twenty-four refrigerators, and that the property should be worth $280,000 but is only worth $260,000 because of my actions.

So you threatened to sue me for the $20,000 difference. Is that a fair summary?"

"Yes, it is."

"Good. Then let me propose this—I will buy the property from you for $280,000 right now."

Silence. "Why would you do that?"

"Look, Jim, you and I were law partners for several years. I've seen you write many letters like this, followed by litigation. So if you file a lawsuit against me we'll probably fight about it for two or three years, I'll spend $20,000 in legal fees, and in the end I might lose. I would prefer to shortcut a dispute and pay you today what you think the property should be worth."

"I'll think about it."

"Fine. Just let me know as soon as you can."

A few days later Jim accepted my offer, and a month or two later I bought his property for $60,000 down and took over the $220,000 loan.

This story has a happy ending. The real estate market was strong, and two years later I sold the same property for $480,000. I earned a profit of $200,000 on my down payment of $60,000. Had I acted impulsively in response to Jim's letter, my cooler head would not have had the chance to prevail—and our happy ending would never have been possible.

Wait Three Days. For fun and profit.

LAUGH

If you want to ruin yourself there are three known ways:
Gambling is the fastest, women are the sweetest,
and banks are the most reliable.
—STAR TREK
Ferengi Rule of Acquisition #185

A man is only worth the sum of his possessions.
—STAR TREK
Ferengi Rule of Acquisition #6

When three distressing events happen to me on the very same day, such as a notice of increased property taxes, a fire at one of my shopping centers, or the resignation of a valued employee, I suspect the universe is out to get me. That's when I give up (temporarily) and laugh. I've noticed that the third catastrophe usually hits about 4:00 p.m., when I'm tired anyway, and which I then consider an excellent time to relax and enjoy myself. It helps when I remember that one hundred years from now (and likely thirty days from now as well) the calamities of today will have melted into the blur of history.

Track and field coaches encourage their sprinters to relax while they're racing to the wire. Evidently this helps them run faster. When I drive I'm in a hurry. My wife is more relaxed about being on time. But when she and I drive separate cars she usually arrives first. It's important for me to remember that to move more swiftly toward my objective, it helps me to loosen up. And it's better for my health.

Norman Cousins famously wrote that when he was in the hospital for a serious condition he watched Marx Brothers films. He said, "I made the joyous discovery that ten minutes of genuine belly laughter had an anesthetic effect and would give me at least two hours of pain-free sleep . . . When the pain-killing effect of the laughter wore off, we would switch on the motion picture projector again and, not infrequently, it would lead to another pain-free interval."

The Mayo Clinic reports, "Whether you're guiltily guffawing at an episode of 'South Park' or quietly giggling at the latest New Yorker cartoon, laughing does you good. Laughter is a great form of stress relief, and that's no joke."

I encourage you to discover what amuses you and use it to improve both your outlook and your productivity. Years ago I found that watching Johnny Carson was a delightful way to end my day. My adult daughters enjoy watching John Stewart.

Years ago I liked the television show *Star Trek: Deep Space Nine*. One of the characters was the lovable Ferengi super-capitalist named Quark. For both a laugh and a Quarky view of business, you might locate the Ferengi Rules of Acquisition on the Internet. (#195: "Wounds heal, but debt is forever." #202a: "A friend in need is a customer in the making." #202b: "A friend in need means three times the profit." And at my semi-advanced age my current personal favorite is #49: "Old age and greed will always overcome youth and talent.")

There will be days when the universe seems to conspire against you. When it does, take a deep breath, give silent thanks that your misfortune wasn't worse, and enjoy a good laugh. And especially if you live by Rule #6, have a good laugh at yourself.

Many of my best laughs are at myself, particularly when I start taking myself (and my problems) too seriously.

A.S.S.

For Kindness begets kindness evermore....
—SOPHOCLES
Ajax

[When asked, "What is a friend?"] Another I.
—ZENO
Diogenes Laertius, Lives of Eminent Philosophers

A.S.S. means After-Sales Service. And if you do not use this People Tool, I'm afraid you are what the acronym spells.

The success of every business is based upon relationships. When I started my commercial real estate company more than forty-five years ago I spent a month raising $5,000 of capital. Today I raise $1,000,000 with one e-mail. Why? Relationships. And these are largely based on After-Sales Service.

Conrad, a former friend, used to visit me only when he wanted something. I realized that I hadn't seen him in several months when he came by one day to ask me for a loan. Notice that I said "former friend."

I have no problem with the idea that we contribute to each other's lives. Each of us is a consumer, a customer, a seller, a friend. But any relationship, in order to endure, must be perceived as approximately equal by both parties most of the time. I realized that my relationship with Conrad was entirely one-sided. He was entertaining, but not that entertaining. I didn't loan him the money, and seldom saw him again.

59

Over the past four decades many people have become investors in the commercial real estate that I buy and manage. I usually earn a profit when the property is bought, and often when a property is sold. But I don't like to "churn" the portfolio. Selling a property after a few years might benefit me, but not necessarily my clients. Transaction costs can gobble up the gain. I once read a book entitled something like, *How I Turned $10,000.00 in the Stock Market into $492.37 in My Spare Time*. The author's mistake was to buy and sell frequently while paying a high transaction cost for every trade. When I hold and manage a property for decades I am providing an After-Sales Service to my investors.

The greatest return on investment often comes with a long-term hold, just as the greatest return from a relationship comes with its longevity. I have co-owned the first shopping center I ever purchased for more than thirty years. It still produces an excellent cash profit and is worth more than six times its purchase price. When the present loan is due I plan to refinance for another ten years. I read recently that Warren Buffet has made two commercial real estate investments in his life, and he still owns both properties.

I have always lost money in property management and have never drawn a salary. My company is profitable through buying and selling, not day-to-day management. Even so, I still spend a great deal of money and time on management, because this is the after-sales service which generates future sales.

From time to time a client will ask my advice on buying a new house or refinancing their present home. I am always happy to help. Without charge. I consider this part of the ongoing service I provide to keep my clients pleased with my services on an ongoing basis.

But let's not confuse A.S.S. with B.S.S. (Before-Sales Service). When I was practicing law and just beginning to buy real estate I met a woman who claimed to be interested in investing with me. I carefully explained to her the ins and outs of investment, and over several years we discussed quite a few specific properties. In turn, she asked me for legal advice every few weeks, which I was happy to give. After almost three years, with no investment forthcoming, she volunteered to pay for my legal services. I accepted her offer and billed her for a small amount when I responded to her next legal question.

The bad news is that she never paid my bill and she never invested with me. The good news is that she never contacted me again to ask for free legal advice.

Not every sales call, or every contact, results in a sale. And each sale does not always produce a profit. I read an article in the *Wall Street Journal* that compared the American style of business to the Asian model. Americans were described as hunters, with the goal of making as much profit as possible from a single kill. The Asian model was more like farming—cultivating the fields of their business relationships.

Today I believe that most successful companies worldwide provide excellent after-sales service. I remember that after a bad experience with another brand of appliances, my mother always bought a Kenmore washer and dryer because of their reputation for reliability and the availability of prompt service. Kenmore must have also impressed my wife with their A.S.S. because we also have a Kenmore washer and dryer in our home.

Jessica, the real estate broker who recently sold to one of my daughters her first home, volunteered to wait one afternoon to meet the service man who was going to turn on the gas. We would certainly use Jessica's services again.

We live today in a service economy, and with a great deal of competition. More than once I have walked out of a restaurant, never to return, because the service was either slow, rude, or both.

It takes a great deal of time and money to obtain one new customer. Why not be careful to retain those you already have? With outstanding A.S.S., you will.

TOOT

He that lives upon hope will die fasting.
—BENJAMIN FRANKLIN
Poor Richard's Almanac

Do you wish people to think well of you?
Don't speak well of yourself.
—BLAISE PASCAL
Pensées

Yes, you are ahead of me again. I am, indeed, talking about Toot, as in "Toot your own horn." But you have to be careful about it. You can't overpower the rest of the orchestra.

I agree, as Pascal advises, that when you brag about yourself people will not think well of you. If a speaker lavishes praise on the donor of an endowed chair at the university I attended, I will applaud. If the speaker then reveals that he is the donor himself, I would promptly sit on my hands. Bragging about yourself is not endearing, but failing to explain your ideas and accomplishments may be worse.

In business, and in life, the question is not, "Should I speak up for myself?" The proper question is how I should speak up for myself, and when. There are times when it is appropriate, or even essential, for you to let others know about your contributions and abilities.

Tim, a colleague of mine in another company, shared with me the following e-mail he received from Beth, the Controller in his business. It serves as a perfect example of someone speaking up for herself without sounding boastful or defensive. I have changed identifying information (and condensed it slightly) but otherwise I have not changed a single word.

From: Beth T.
Sent: Monday, December 06, 2013 10:18 a.m.
To: Tim G.
Subject: Feedback from Staff

Tim,

I truly appreciate that you listened to my concerns and gave me good advice. Thank you for providing a safe environment that encourages openness and honesty. I try to do the same for my staff. You said that you knew I was good at accounting but cannot attest to my managerial skill as you haven't seen it firsthand. I appreciate your candor and thought to provide some feedback from key people in my department. Lou and Linda are my top performers and I truly value what they think so I'd like to share their feedback with you. I have worked with Elizabeth very closely during her time here. We had our disagreements but worked through them. We enjoyed mutual respect and open communication, thereby cultivating a good working relationship.

Linda R. (A/R Supervisor): Quoted from self-evaluation
"I feel Beth and I have developed a great relationship. She keeps her door open and I think we both benefit from having a colleague to brainstorm with to work towards resolving the variety of issues as they arise."

Lou W. (Promoted from A/P to CAM Specialist): Paraphrased from a verbal conversation
Lou told me that one major factor towards his accepting the CAM position is that this is the calmest, smoothest, no-drama CAM season that he's ever experienced in his 9 years at the company and he credited me for it. I thanked him and said it was a team effort and I'm glad that we were successful in making it happen.

Elizabeth M. (CAM Specialist): Quoted from exit interview
"Beth was wonderful to work with—amazing to watch in action with her grasp of everything going on around her in her financial/finances world with the ability to jump from one

area to the next without missing a beat along with an excellent work ethic—and I was fortunate that we got along extremely well, even at the most stressful time (i.e., CAM season)!"

I still have many things to learn as a manager but I know that I am growing and doing good work along the way.

Best regards,
Beth T.
Controller

Was Beth bragging? No. Was she giving her boss a clear idea of how she was perceived by three of the employees she supervised? Yes. Will she do well in whatever company is fortunate enough to employ her? You tell me. I would love to hire Beth.

My writing teachers have always repeated the writing refrain, "Show me, don't tell me."

Beth has shown us an excellent Toot. I'm going to move on and demonstrate something important in the next chapter.

THE HIDDEN AGENDA

My younger brother David was a very successful man. He won the Moot Court Competition at Stanford Law School. He served as Real Estate Commissioner for the State of California and wrote the real estate ethics law, which remains in effect today. Then David became a licensed family therapist, and for ten years he brilliantly trained interns to successfully take the MFCC oral and written examinations. But far more important to me, David was a loving and supportive brother.

I remember a lawsuit in which my deposition was being taken. The opposing attorney seemed to believe that if he was extremely nasty he could goad me into making a mistake. Instead, he provoked my brother David, who was at my side, into blasting his questioning into a pile of rubble. I should mention that David served for several years as an Assistant U.S. Attorney and was not afraid of anyone. I saw him answer back, appropriately, to one autocratic Federal District Judge who threatened David with contempt and jail time. Confronting a deposing attorney who was trying to bully me was child's play for David, and both a comfort and a joy for me.

Early in his career David worked for me. Twice. The first time I hired him to work as an attorney in my law firm. While he was an excellent litigator, David spent far more time on each case than I was able to bill to clients, and in the name of staying in business I had to let him go.

A few years later I hired David to work on acquisitions for my real estate company. He never seemed to like the fundamentals of the position, and eventually began to appear in his office for fewer and fewer hours each week. One day the two of us visited a therapist together to work out our differences. This was in the days before e-mails and cell phones simplified the exchange of information.

After some discussion, I found myself saying, "David. I need to communicate with you. I need to know what is going on. The minimum I can accept is for you to be at your desk in my offices from ten until noon Monday through Thursday. That's eight hours a week."

"I can't promise to do that," he said.

"You're fired."

I was surprised at my sudden decision. I think all three of us were. But I realized that if David would not commit to eight hours a week at his desk he really didn't want the job. Our half-hour drive back to the office was like a joint trip to the San Quentin death chamber.

Why did David refuse to commit to being available eight hours a week? We discussed this question many years later, and David admitted that he had been uncomfortable with the job, but did not want to disappoint me by quitting. In short, his agenda was to leave, but he kept that hidden from me, and even from himself.

I have witnessed the same dynamic in more than one marriage. The unhappy spouse wants to get out but is unwilling to give his or her partner the bad news. So Mr. or Mrs. Unhappy behaves in such a way that his or her partner initiates a separation or divorce.

Beware of hidden agendas. If you want in or out of a relationship you should consider being courageous and saying just that. You will save two people months or years of misery, and both of you will be able to go on with your lives. If someone else has a hidden agenda with you, revealed only by his or her actions or inactions, you would be better off initiating a split sooner rather than later. After all, you really aren't together while the hidden agenda keeps you apart.

After more than ten years with me, Gloria, one of my outstanding accounting employees, left for an exceptional opportunity in a larger company. But after three weeks in her new position Gloria came to see me.

"My new boss seems threatened by me, refuses to give me information I need, and then criticizes me for my ignorance." In Gloria's case (and in most) it is very important to remember that ignorance is not the same as stupidity, especially when you are seeking the information that you need to do a better job.

"Does your boss want you to leave?"

"I think so," she said, "but I need the income. I can't afford to quit."

Gloria remained for another two months, until she finally was fired. I hired her back for temporary work, but soon she found an even better new job.

A hidden agenda, whether yours or someone else's, will bite you every time.

I have one final word about David. When he was sixty, three months before he died of a sudden and unexpected heart attack, he wrote the following note to himself:

"DF ENJOYING HIS LIFE

"3/18/13

"I am happy now because I know I have a wonderful future to live because I am in charge. No one else is in charge of my future!!! No one can stop me from living my wonderful future—not even me!!!

"YEAH"

I am happy that my brother's hidden agenda came to light and didn't keep him from ultimately finding his well-deserved happiness.

BE A CONTRARIAN

If a man does not keep pace with his companions, perhaps it is because he hears a different drummer. Let him step to the music which he hears, however measured or far away.

—HENRY DAVID THOREAU
Walden

Your system was liable to periodical convulsions . . . business crises at intervals of five to ten years, which wrecked the industries of the nation.

—EDWARD BELLAMY
Looking Backward, 2000-1887

Sir Isaac Newton wrote, "Every body continues in its state of rest, or of uniform motion in a right line, unless it is compelled to change that state by forces impressed upon it."

Sir Isaac thought he was talking about physics. I think he was talking about business expectations.

Many business projections, and a majority of business decisions, are based upon the recent past. We each expect that whatever we have experienced lately will continue indefinitely. When business has been good for two years in a row we assume that next year will be even better and that the year after that will be fabulous. When many people lose their jobs we worry about losing our job, we spend less, and as a result more people, possibly including us, become underemployed or unemployed. As the joke goes, a recession is when you lose your job. A depression is when I lose mine.

The best prediction I ever heard about the stock market was attributed to Bernard Baruch, who made his fortune by investing in stocks. When asked whether he expected the market to go up or to go down he said, "It will fluctuate."

This is precisely the point—the business cycle will fluctuate, but seldom when we expect it to. The majority is almost always wrong, and it's tough to swim against the tide. Fortunately, my father raised me to be a contrarian. "If everyone is buying, then sell," he said. "If everyone is selling, then it's time to buy."

My father once called his stockbroker, Carr Neel Miller, and asked for his company's research on First Charter Financial Corporation. Mr. Miller said, "Fred, the Savings and Loan industry is so shaky that E. F. Hutton & Co. doesn't even follow it. We have no research."

My father smiled and bought 4,000 shares of First Charter Financial at $7.00 a share. Four years later, when brokerage houses were heartily recommending the stock, my dad sold First Charter at $28.00 a share. That's a profit of 300 percent in four years. I would say this is an excellent example of how using the tool of contrary thinking can work to your advantage.

I have faced exactly the same situation in my field. I started buying and selling commercial real estate in 1968. At that time I was told that the commercial real estate market had been weak for the last five years, and I was foolish to even consider that kind of investment. I smiled and began to invest. The market soon improved dramatically.

In 1980 I met a high school teacher at a party. He told me he was in escrow to buy two condominiums because, "I can flip them each at a 20 percent profit, even before I close escrow. Real estate is a great way to make money."

I stopped buying real estate for two years. I felt that the roller-coaster business cycle was at its peak, and I didn't want to be there for the inevitable fall.

The best stock investor of our time, Warren Buffet, has been reported to say, "When others get greedy, I get scared. When others get scared, I get greedy."

Of course, most of my investors are not contrarians. They will invest heavily when the market has been strong for three or four years, and invest reluctantly, if at all, when the market has been weak for a year or two. As I have said, "We each expect that whatever we have experienced lately will continue indefinitely."

I say that business, and life itself, is not likely to travel in a straight line forever. As Newton observed in the quotation at the start of this chapter, ". . . unless it is compelled to change that state by forces impressed upon it." The force impressed upon the economy might be as simple as Lehmann Brothers filing for bankruptcy on September 15, 2008, or as complex as the interplay of new technology and a change of government regimes in sixteen different countries. But change itself is inevitable.

Be prepared. Consider being a contrarian. In business and, perhaps, in life.

This idea is summed up by Robert Frost in his poem "The Road Not Taken."

> I shall be telling this with a sigh
> Somewhere ages and ages hence
> Two roads diverged in a wood, and I—
> I took the road less traveled by,
> And that has made all the difference.

PEOPLE TOOL
18
FOR BUSINESS

GIVE IT AWAY

Common Sense is not so common.

—VOLTAIRE
Dictionaire Philosophique

Friends share all things.

—PYTHAGORAS
From Diogenes Laertius, Lives of Eminent Philosophers

I am working at my desk. I hear a soft chime, and up pops an e-mail from one of my investors. He's asking me a question. He has asked me this same question three times during the past two months and yet I continue to avoid answering him because I know that it would take me an hour to research and respond. Now my investor is upset and I am under increasing pressure to perform. What to do, what to do?

I have a minor "aha!" moment. Instead of doing the research myself, I forward my investor's request to my assistant, Yana, with a note, "Please prepare a draft." That takes me only ten seconds, and the investor's question is now on its way to being answered.

I've been in business for more than fifty years. For most of that time I've been the president of my own company. Why in the world have I still failed to master the simple art of delegating, which I prefer to call "giving it away"?

Now that I'm consciously thinking about it, I find a number of reasons why I still cling to tasks when I should simply give them away. Here are my reasons. I'm not saying they are good reasons.

1. Ego. Despite thousands of occasions in which I have successfully delegated a task, which often was performed better by someone else, I still believe unconsciously that I can do a better job than anyone.

2. Cost. I pay Yana for her time and I am cost conscious. I irrationally flinch at the idea of using Yana's time, while ignoring the fact that my time is actually more valuable to me.

3. Timing. Even with ample evidence to the contrary, I still do not trust others to follow through in a timely way. Ironically, my failure to promptly "give it away" usually causes a much longer delay than if I had delegated immediately.

4. Ignorance. Dumb and dumber. Like many people, when I don't know what to do, I do nothing. Of course, this means that the problem is left to grow like an aggressive cancer.

5. Fear of rejection. I often fear that any answer or action will offend someone who will then reject me in some way. On a deep level I am still terrified of potential rejection.

6. Wishful thinking. If I don't act, maybe the problem will disappear, and I will never have to do anything. Wouldn't that be nice? Sometimes the problem actually does disappear, which reinforces my inclination to procrastinate.

7. The easy way out. I often imagine that there is a quick and easy answer, which I will think of tomorrow or next week.

Yet I have often given away both responsibility and authority during my business career, and with undeniable success. This is what has worked for me:

1. Give away the ENTIRE task. Nearly twenty years ago I began to publish *Rattle*, a poetry magazine. I have employed two editors to help me out and, in essence, run the journal for me. First, I hired Stellasue Lee who worked very hard to put the word out that we were accepting submissions and built up our subscriber base. She then helped me to hire her successor, our present editor, Tim Green. Tim is incredible. He has created an outstanding website with a new poem posted daily and has created monthly poetry readings for *Rattle* poets. He personally works with a number of poets whose poems are very close to being accepted for publication by *Rattle*, but are not quite good enough yet.

   Every two weeks Tim and I review those poems that he thinks are worthy of consideration. I sign checks and approve his new ideas. Tim does everything else. Thanks to the help of these two brilliant editors, *Rattle* works, so I don't have to. By comparison, my poetry mentor (who encouraged me to launch *Rattle*) publishes his own poetry journal, but he does all the work himself. As a result, often several years go by before his subscribers receive a new issue of his journal.

2. Pay for help. I don't try to cut my own hair. I delegate that task to someone who has the equipment and expertise to do a proper job. Yana has gradually assumed the role of talking to our investors. Just because I can do something, or just because I have performed a particular task for years, does not mean that I should be doing it today.

3. Trust. There are many people in the world who are just as good as I am at solving problems. I have entrusted

Kat with the responsibility of marketing my writing. I do the writing, show up at appearances, and direct overall strategy. She does the work she is trained for, good at, and loves.

4. Accept a blemish. Hindsight is grand. I can virtually always improve on a process or performance when I review it later. So can you. And it's easy for each of us to believe that if we had performed the work in the first place it would have been better. Don't believe that. Imperfections will exist no matter who does the job.

5. Get past perfect. This is tool #16 in my original *People Tools* book. I determined long ago that in business I would settle for being a failed perfectionist. If I needed this book to be perfect you wouldn't be reading it because, in my opinion, it is not and never will be perfect. Relax and enjoy your life, warts and all. If my wife were, in fact, perfect, she probably wouldn't want me. (Or maybe she is perfect because she does.)

I am filled with a sense of both relief and fear every time I "give it away." From now on I'm going to focus on the relief, and let go of my attachment to the fear.

When a new task pops up in my inbox, my first reaction will not be "I'll take another look at this tomorrow." Instead, my first thought will be, "Can I give this away?" My next thought will be "to whom?"

PEOPLE TOOL 19 FOR BUSINESS

I AND THOU

Human felicity is produced not so much by great pieces of good fortune that seldom happen, as by little advantages that occur every day.
—BENJAMIN FRANKLIN
Autobiography

A little rule, a little sway,
A sunbeam in a winter's day,
Is all the proud and mighty have
Between the cradle and the grave.
—JOHN DYER
Grongar Hill

I have begun to read Martin Buber's seminal book *I and Thou* twice. Each time I gave up on the third page. I've made the effort, but to me Buber's philosophy is both challenging and very dense. Fortunately, I don't think we have to read his treatise to appreciate the beauty of the concept he embraces.

As I understand it, Buber's central idea is that in our lives we can either think of everything outside our skin as an object that is separate from us ("It"), or we can realize that we have a relationship with people and things outside our skin and see them as not separated from us by discrete boundaries ("Thou"). A major theme of Martin's book is that we find meaning in relationships, not in objects, and that humans are defined by two word pairs: *I-It* and *I-Thou*.

At age three I was devastated when my teddy bear, which I had transformed from an "it" into a treasured "thou," and was dirty and ragged from years of my loving embrace, suddenly disappeared. I'm not pointing a finger at my parents, and I now understand the value of hygiene, but I still recreate my teddy bear with a pillow every night before I fall asleep. Cuddling with my wife, of course, is an excellent substitute.

Tool #27 in the original *People Tools* is called "Things Are Only Things," for good reason. I do not spend my emotional energy on things. Things can be repaired or replaced. People cannot. So I reserve my emotional energy for people. And in communicating my caring and respect for other people I pay attention to my own People Tools.

As Mark Twain observed, "The difference between the *almost right* word and the *right word* is really a large matter—'tis the difference between the lightning-bug and the lightening."*

I often write business letters to my investors. For the past forty years I have used first names in business letters and e-mails. It's always "Dear Carl," rather than "Dear Mr. Smith." Also, when a building is performing poorly I refer to it as "the" building. When it's performing well it becomes "our" building. *I-It* turns into *I-Thou*.

I remember numbers easily. I have difficulty recalling names, but I always make an effort. Years ago I read that the new CEO of United Airlines, Richard Ferris, spent months flying around the world on United, talking to employees—from pilots to baggage handlers to mechanics. He met and remembered the names of thousands of his workers. Good for Richard, who recognized his coworkers as *I-Thou* rather than *I-It*. I have fewer than one hundred employees. Though I still don't know everyone's name, I am always trying to learn. I use first names whenever I can, and they use mine. Each time someone contributes an idea or information of value in a conversation, I respond with "Thank you, Helen," or "Good idea, Bob."

When you value another human being, which I hope is often, an *I-Thou* approach goes a long way toward establishing or maintaining

---

* Letter to George Bainton, 15 October 1888, solicited for and printed in George Bainton, *The Art of Authorship: Literary Reminiscences, Methods of Work, and Advice to Young Beginners* (1890), pp. 87–88.

a nurturing, enjoyable, and enduring relationship. Every one of us is a living, breathing, feeling human being.

Recently Linzi Levinson was interviewing me on her radio show *Illuminating Now!* She told me that several days earlier she was at her local Baskin Robbins buying ice cream for her daughter. The husky seventeen-year-old-boy behind the counter had been treating customers rudely, and after Linzi paid he "frisbeed my credit card across the room and under a table." Linzi retrieved her credit card and returned to the counter. Every eye in the store, including her daughter's, was focused on her.

"It looks like you're having a really bad day," she said to the boy.

"Yes. I have a badly sprained wrist. It hurts a lot every time I scoop the ice cream. I asked for the day off, but my boss said I had to work." The boy was close to tears.

"I'm so sorry. Not being listened to must hurt even more than your wrist."

Now the boy did shed tears. He responded to Linzi's *I-Thou* by giving both her and her daughter a few "extras," and providing outstanding service to the rest of the customers in the store.

I and Thou.

Both business and life are all about *I-Thou* relationships, which not only connect us to each other but also give our lives meaning. By treating others with care and compassion we make life better not only for ourselves, but also for everyone we meet. That's good business. I will return when my barber greets me by name.

The Dalai Lama said, "This is my simple religion. There is no need for temples; no need for complicated philosophy. Our own brain, our own heart is our temple; the philosophy is kindness."

PEOPLE TOOL
20
FOR BUSINESS

IGNORE

Here I am, an old man in a dry month,
Being read to by a boy, waiting for rain.
—THOMAS STEARNS ELIOT
Gerontion

A man cannot be too careful in the choice of his enemies.
—OSCAR WILDE
The Critic as Artist

I have never in my life intentionally made a serious enemy, and as far as I know I don't have any. That does not mean that I have not been the target of hostility, some of it rather unpleasant. When I am emotionally distressed I use the People Tool for Business of Wait Three Days. But when I'm just disturbed, not dismayed, I simply ignore the invective and respond, if at all, to the substance. This doesn't happen often, but when it does I have the chance to walk my talk.

Several years ago I had a serious policy conflict with Judith, the CEO of one of my retail businesses, and asked her to take early retirement. Judith's husband, Richard, had been an investor of mine and was offended by my asking his wife to retire. Without telling Judith he sent me an extremely hostile e-mail. In it he attacked my character, questioned my competence, and told me in a rather profane way what he thought of me and the situation. He then told me he wanted to immediately liquidate all of his investments.

I was out of my office when I received his malicious missive, and was without immediate access to my business records. But in the interest of helping him calm down, I promptly sent the following response.

> Richard,
>
> Thank you for your e-mail. I have a strict policy of doing my best to meet an investor's request for liquidation, and when that direction comes in the form of a definite instruction, I do not offer comment.
>
> I will prepare and forward to you a computation of the amount of the present estimated equity in your investments. I strongly recommend that you consult with your own income tax advisor(s) regarding any potential income tax or other financial implications. Upon your approval of the actual amounts, I will prepare and forward documentation. As soon as that is returned to my office, fully executed, I will wire funds.
>
> Alan

Using the tool of Ignore, I made sure I didn't react to his highly insulting e-mail, and I made a point to eliminate my emotions from my response. Ironically, several days later my vice president in charge of investor relations told me that Richard had liquidated all of his investments long before he indulged in this invective toward me.

A short time later we held a very nice retirement party for his wife Judith. Richard attended and was quite cordial. We have seen each other several times since, and even hugged goodbye recently. When you ignore the hostility, bygones eventually really do become bygones.

When I began my weekly blog I sent emails to all of my present and past investors and business partners to interest them in subscribing. One unexpected response, which I deleted after I answered it, said something like, "Pardon me if I don't kneel down and kiss your ring. You didn't even ask about how my family is doing."

My answer (which I wish I hadn't sent): "My ring is pretty tarnished by now. And I hope that your family is doing really well." Then I permanently deleted the e-mail address from my records.

There are two situations in which you should use the People Tool of Ignore.

First, when you're offended, and especially when you're highly offended, do not send an inflammatory response. If you would feel better you can write it, print it out, and even share it with your best friend or your spouse. Then tear it up. Why bother sending it and potentially creating a real enemy? We all need friends in this world, not infuriated foes.

Second, use Ignore when you receive a bitter communication, especially if it is delivered in person. Ignore the tirade, respond to the business part if you wish, and have a really nice day anyway.

I've been working for years to apply the following proverb to my life:

"Living well is the best revenge."

I suggest we all live well.

PEOPLE TOOLS FOR BUSINESS

21

CHARACTER IS COSTUME

Be valiant, but not too venturous.
Let thy attire be comely, but not costly.

—JOHN LYLY
Euphues: The Anatomy of Wit

I'll give my jewels for a set of beads,
My gorgeous palace for a hermitage,
My gay apparel for an almsman's gown.

—SHAKESPEARE
King Richard the Second

I'm a devotee of numbers, of margins and percentages, of profit and loss. But no matter how important the statistics, ultimately I think of business in terms of people—customers, employees, managers, owners, investors. Every one of them is an individual who is trying the best he or she can to enjoy a happy life.

And each of us starts with appearance. We know that to make a favorable impression we need to be as attractive as we can. We may think that we need to drive the right car, live in the right neighborhood, or have the right office. But being attractive is so much more than what we present to other people on the outside. It is also how we feel about ourselves on the inside.

When I first saw Daveen out of the corner of my eye more than thirty-five years ago I thought, "Wow." My immediate enthusiasm may have been based in part by her appearance, but even more by her demeanor—the way she sat, and the look in her eye as she worked at her desk at the rare books store where I was a customer.

Each of us wears clothing that can offer exterior clues about our wealth, status, and self-image. For me clothing is most important for comfort and protection, not to impress others. I wear shirts with long sleeves to avoid sunburn, dark slacks, which are always in fashion except at the beach, and shoes which are comfortable. Forty years ago I stopped wearing ties, except for the occasional trip to a fancy restaurant, a wedding of a close friend, or an appearance in court.

My clothes are part of my costume, but only a part. The rest of my costume is me. Indeed, a clean, decent appearance is an excellent start, especially in business, but I'm more concerned with the rest of your costume. The "you" inside your body and inside your head. Your feelings, your thoughts, your character.

Last week I mentioned to my yoga teacher that I want to lose more weight. At the end of my lesson she asked me to lie on my back on the yoga mat, close my eyes, and visualize my body weighing 165 pounds. I did.

I saw myself as a very small man. And I want to be big, because I equate size with importance, influence, and respect. I don't ever want to be that proverbial 97-pound weakling with a bully kicking sand in my face at the beach.

In just two minutes, after more than seventy years of soul-searching, I discovered why, aside from ingrained eating habits, I have always been large. I don't want to be invisible. I want to count. That's my emotional side. But I also realized that, as Thomas Henry Huxley put it, "Size is not grandeur, and territory does not make a nation."

I'm told that Bruce Lee weighed 135 pounds. Gandhi would often fast to develop his moral power, not his physical stature. Bill Gates, the richest man in the world, looks like a nerd. (Bill—please don't take offense. I mean that fondly. I like the look.)

Last week I was a guest on a radio talk show. A female listener asked the question, "I am a twenty-six-year-old single law student.

I'm reasonably good looking, but the only women men in Los Angeles seem to want to date are beauty queens."

I have a poor memory for specific dialogue, and don't remember what I actually said. What I would like to have said is this: Anyone and everyone who can and will help you in life will see through your exterior and into your character. You don't need Aesop from 550 B.C. to tell you "Appearances often are deceiving." You know that. I know that. Most of us, in our hearts, know that.

I agree with John Lyly—spend your most precious time and passion to create a beautiful character, rather than a transitory costume. This is true in business. And this is also true in all other aspects of life.

Your character is the costume that will fit you perfectly and serve you well for the rest of your life. Wear it comfortably. And if I can revise my habits around food, you might find me looking more like an elder Bruce Lee than the Incredible Hulk.

PEOPLE TOOL
22
FOR BUSINESS

DON'T SUE THE BASTARD

*Lawsuit, (n.) a machine which you go into as a pig
and come out as a sausage.*

—AMBROSE BIERCE
The Devil's Dictionary

*And do as adversaries do in law,
Strive mightily, but eat and drink as friends.*

—SHAKESPEARE
The Taming of the Shrew

According to Wikipedia there were 30,516 attorneys registered
with bar associations in Japan as of March 1, 2011. That is far fewer
than the more than 180,000 lawyers registered to actively practice
law in the State of California.

I have lived and worked in California my entire life. You should
not be surprised to learn that during the past fifty years I have been
involved in a number of lawsuits. Most have involved the collection
of rent. A few have been more serious. From my personal experience
I have drawn the following conclusions about Sue the Bastard, which
refers to the use of litigation.

First, actively avoid people and companies that are known to be
litigious. Patterns, as I wrote in *People Tools*, tend to persist. I once
purchased several businesses from a sizeable Dallas investment company. Within six months the investment company managers sued me
in two states. This may have been a pattern of theirs.

Second, a bad settlement is better than a good lawsuit. Most cases are settled before trial, and should be.

I was once sued by a billion-dollar construction firm in Northern California. They claimed that I owed them $72,000. I knew they owed me $20,000. Even though I thought I was right, I called the CEO of my adversary to make an offer of settlement.

"You claim that I owe you $72,000," I said. "My position is that, at worst, I owe you nothing. It will cost each of us about $35,000 to litigate the case and under our agreement the winner cannot recover attorney fees. I propose that I pay you $36,000 now to settle the case."

"No. I won't accept $36,000."

"Okay. What amount will you accept?"

"The full amount due: $72,000."

I was startled.

"But if you win you will recover $72,000 and pay about $35,000 in attorney fees. So there is no way you can come out of this with more than about $37,000."

"I will not settle for less than the full amount due."

He was clear. I wanted to settle, but this was sounding like a waste of my energy.

"Thanks for your time," I said. "If you change your mind please let me know."

"I won't."

Almost a year later we went into a trial in which I wasted two days of my life. The judge ordered me to pay $38,000. I have no idea where he extracted that number, but he did. I paid that amount, plus about $35,000 to my own attorney for legal fees. This adventure cost me $73,000. The giant construction company received $38,000, less their legal fees, which must have been about the same as mine. The result was that their lawsuit netted them no more than $3,000.

As I said, settle. If you need help arriving at settlement terms or the opposing party is difficult (and don't we always think they are), mediation can be quite helpful. But, if at all possible, settle before you spend every cent you have on legal fees and costs.

Dickens' novel *Bleak House* tells the tale of a protracted lawsuit over an inheritance. At the end of the book the case is finally dismissed. No one receives any money since the inheritance had been entirely consumed by the legal fees. In litigation, this result is not uncommon.

Third, large corporations tend to be litigation bullies. They believe they can win by intimidation, and often they are right. I once loaned my friend Edgar a substantial amount to finance his legal fees when a large foreign firm failed to keep its agreement and nearly bankrupted his company. They didn't care. Edgar eventually paid back a part of the money I had loaned to him.

Fourth, the better attorney wins. I like to save money and tend to use the lowest or second-lowest bidder. In two areas this approach does not work very well. In replacing roofs you want the most reliable contractor, not the cheapest. Once I hired the cheapest roofer and in the next rainstorm my new roof leaked even more than the old roof. In litigation you want the best attorney you can hire, and the best is not always the most expensive. Look into reputation and results as well as personal recommendations.

In litigating with the investment company over our business transaction, I hired a brilliant New York City law firm. After more than a year of expensive court battles we ended up involved in settlement negotiations. Ultimately we were successful and settled the case. I regard that as a victory for both sides. Very few litigants really win. Their attorneys often earn a very good living.

Fifth, all litigation is emotionally draining. A friend of mine was involved in bitter divorce litigation (and most divorce litigation is bitter). Although he made a reasonable offer to settle, his wife was uncertain how to proceed. For that reason she did not even respond to his offer. As a result, when the divorce went to trial my friend had to reveal all of his financial information in court. The litigation consumed a full year of two lives—six lives if you count the children. It was emotionally draining for both parties to prepare for and participate in a protracted trial, where the outcome was uncertain.

Henry, a doctor I know, was sued for malpractice. He found it emotionally difficult to continue practicing medicine, and focused his entire life on the legal action until it was settled more than a year after it had begun.

Sixth, sympathy prevails and judges and juries are fickle. When I graduated from law school I was certain that litigation was straightforward. You put in the facts, apply the law, and every judge will come to the same conclusion—that you are the winner. My original thinking was a complete delusion.

I was involved years ago in a dispute with a tenant who claimed that he was not properly served with the summons and complaint. At the first hearing the judge told me that I was a bad person and would surely lose. For procedural reasons, he set the hearing in another judge's courtroom for exactly one week later, and strongly advised me to settle before that hearing. I did not agree with the first judge.

During the following week we did not settle. The file the second judge read was exactly the same file submitted to the first judge. And yet one week later the new judge told the tenant that he was a bad person, that I had been more than fair, and I won.

My point is that an outcome in court depends upon the judge (or the jury) and not so much upon either the facts or the law. In 2000 George W. Bush won the presidency in a 5-4 ruling by the United States Supreme Court, in what most observers described as a political decision. I am not commenting on that decision, only on how easily it could have gone the other way. I am just pointing out how our legal system actually operates. There is a reason that banks insist in their contracts that a dispute will not be tried before a jury. A jury will most likely sympathize with the little guy, and not the bank.

Sue the bastard? I don't think so. Not if you can avoid it.

PEOPLE TOOL 23 FOR BUSINESS

EMOTION TRUMPS INTELLECT

I joked about every prominent man in my lifetime,
but I never met one I didn't like.

—WILL ROGERS
Epitaph

The brain may devise laws for the blood,
but a hot temper leaps o'er a cold decree

—SHAKESPEARE
The Merchant of Venice

Every decision you make, whether to move to Alaska or to forego bread at dinner, is based upon your emotions, your intellect, or a combination of both. My own decisions are based upon my emotions, verified by my intellect. When the decision is a close one, I reach the more enduring result when I allow my feelings to prevail. One evening I brought this idea up with my dad.

"This time you're dead wrong," he said. My dad and I have enjoyed a running difference of opinion on many issues for years. When I told him I was writing about how I thought "Emotion Trumps Intellect," Dad categorically disagreed with my premise. He believes that intellect trumps emotion.

My friend, David Beaird, is a noted director. When we attended one of his plays together there was a large reproduction of two reviews in the lobby. One was favorable, the other unfavorable. The reviews were headed by the director's statement on top, "You decide."

That is an effective strategy, so I'm going to present both sides of our argument and let you decide.

When my son Craig moved to Raleigh-Durham he asked me to help him find a home. On the first day of looking the realtor showed us seven houses. That evening Craig said, "Dad, you didn't express an opinion on any of the houses we saw today. Did you like any of them?"

"Craig, your job is to find a house you love. You're going to live in it, not me. If I love it and you don't, you shouldn't buy it. If you love it, then I'll give you my opinion and help you with the real estate details. Until you find a house you love my opinion is irrelevant."

The next day we did see a house that Craig loved (you can read more about this house in the foreword Craig wrote for *People Tools* and in the chapter describing People Tool #40 "After You, Gaston"). It was for sale by the owner. I believe that when you find something, or someone you love, go for it immediately. I insisted that we visit the owner that evening. Craig presented an offer, the owner negotiated, and in an hour we agreed on the terms of a sale. Emotion Trumps Intellect.

Last weekend at the Los Angeles Book Festival, my daughter Jill saw a rescue dog she instantly loved. Jill's family already owned two dogs, but she has seldom loved a dog at first sight before. That dog now lives with her in Northern California. Emotion triumphed.

Years ago Daveen and I were invited to dinner at the home of a friend. He wanted us to meet his new wife. She cooked an excellent dinner, the conversation was lively, and their hospitality pleasant.

On our drive home I turned to Daveen and said, "I don't like her." "Why not?"

I thought about it. I remembered first seeing Daveen out of the corner of my eye years before at her place of work. At that time I said to myself, "Wow. I could love that woman." I didn't know if she was married or single. I only felt "Wow." No intellect. Just emotion.

My reaction to my friend's new wife was similar. No intellect, just emotion. "I don't know. She was entirely agreeable, dinner was perfectly pleasant, but I just don't like her and I don't know why." I still don't. Emotion Trumps Intellect.

I once traveled to Stockton, California, to inspect an apartment complex I had agreed to buy.

My father invested in two apartment buildings when I was young. He always said to me, "Look at the numbers first. Never be seduced by 'pride of ownership.' If the numbers work, make an offer. Take a look at the property once you have a deal." My dad's advice has been extremely valuable. When buying commercial real estate I keep my emotions out of the decision until after my intellect has evaluated the investment.

And over the years my dad's advice has helped me avoid the emotional trap we all can fall into of "I want this now."

I have now spent forty-five years buying and selling commercial real estate. Once I did not follow my father's advice and I visited the property first. It was the lovely 301 unit Governor's Square apartments in downtown Sacramento. I liked it so much that I agreed to buy it at the asking price. I overpaid, lost money, and was lucky to get most of my investment back when I sold it three or four years later. This is the perfect example of a situation where I should NOT have let my emotions trump my intellect.

And that is why I had negotiated in advance a price and terms before I traveled to Stockton to inspect the apartment complex. I wanted to avoid another situation in which my emotions trumped my intellect.

As the real estate broker parked his car in front of the property I stared at the exterior walls. They reminded me of a penitentiary.

"I'm not going to buy this property," I said.

"But Alan, you've come all the way from Los Angeles, you've negotiated a great price. At least you should get out of the car and spend half an hour to take a closer look."

That was good salesmanship, and relationships are important to me. I was also curious to see if my first impression would endure after a full inspection. At the end of a forty-five minute tour of the apartment complex my emotion moved from dislike to disgust. I hated the property and cancelled my purchase on the spot.

Might this have been an excellent investment? I'll never know. I didn't buy it, even though the numbers were great. But my emotion, once again, trumped my intellect.

My dad will be one hundred years old in a few months, and has always lived by his principles. A few months ago he told me that he had read a newspaper article about Nelson Mandela, Mahatma Gandhi, and Will Rogers.

"The article said that all three of these great men had one thing in common. They didn't bear grudges. When Mandela came into power he did not show any resentment toward those who had imprisoned him for twenty-seven years."

Then my dad announced, "I'm going to do the same. I'm not going to carry around grudges anymore."

And, as always, his Belt Buckle (what he does) has matched his words.

Dad's intellect trumped, or at least quarantined, his emotion. My father made a conscious decision to actively begin practicing the art of forgiveness and as a result no longer bears a grudge against anyone. My father is quite good at following his own prescribed course of action. His longevity must be, at least in part, a testament to his eliminating emotional stress from his life as a result. The man still has all of his wits, and I enjoy his company—including our running disagreements. True to his word, Dad has learned to forgive and has now become much more complimentary and mellow even though when I was young he was a firebrand.

Can intellect trump emotion? Should emotion overrule intellect? There are situations where a case could be made for either view. But ultimately these are questions which each of us must answer for him- or herself in every situation. As my friend the director said, "You decide." But choose intentionally. Don't let emotions adversely impact sound business judgment, but don't allow your intellect to prevent your finding joy in your life.

DON'T PUT YOUR CAR KEYS
IN THE TRUNK

Experience is the name everyone gives to their mistakes.
—OSCAR WILDE
Lady Windemere's Fan, Act III

I have but one lamp by which my feet are guided,
and that is the lamp of experience.
I know no way of judging of the future but by the past.
—PATRICK HENRY, SPEECH IN VIRGINIA
Convention, Richmond, March, 23, 1775

I like to be efficient. Mistakes are wasteful, so I have developed a number of rules in my business toolbox to keep me from making time-consuming or costly mistakes. There is a very good reason for each rule, as I sometimes learn, to my regret, when I fail to follow them.

Many years ago I was in Beverly Hills and returned to my car with a large box I needed to put into the trunk. This was before the age of remote controls which now open and close most everything. I used my key to open the trunk.

My rule, of course, which I never break, is: WHEN YOU OPEN THE TRUNK TO YOUR CAR, NEVER PUT THE KEYS INSIDE.

I have a reason for that rule, and you know what that reason is. This time, as I put my keys on the floor of the trunk, the smart voice inside my head said, "You're breaking the rule." The stupid voice said, "It's okay. You'll remember and take the keys out before you . . . "

Slam! I remembered my keys just as the descending trunk reached the point of no return.

I called the auto club. Oops. I had a model of car which they couldn't break into. My wife was at work in Burbank. I called her. She had the other set of keys. It took her an hour and a half to arrive.

A few years later I was leaving for a two-week vacation. I didn't want to carry my keys with me, but since other people would be in my house I hid them. I hid those keys so well that I couldn't find them when I returned. I had to replace every single key at a high cost of time, money, and aggravation. Two years later I found them at the back of the high shelf in my closet, just out of view.

What have I learned?

1. My toolbox rules for efficiency exist for good reason. Follow them.

2. Don't put your car keys in the trunk of your car. Ever.

3. If you hide anything out of sight, write down its location. I always forget the hiding place.

4. If it's important, keep duplicates nearby. In plain view.

From age forty-five to forty-seven it became more and more difficult for me to read anything. I'm a guy, so I didn't ask for help. When I was squinting at letters and memos and reading them with difficulty, I finally visited a doctor. He said my eyesight was basically fine but suggested that I buy reading glasses. I did. Within two days I lost the glasses.

Today, if you looked, you would find reading glasses in my shirt pocket, my pants pocket, my wife's purse, the bathroom, the kitchen table (two pairs—I sometimes walk off with one pair and I really like to read the morning newspaper), my desk (many pairs), my briefcase, my suitcase, and my car (not in the trunk). My wife told me the other day that she has another pair in her car, just in case.

In business it is also important to be efficient and avoid mistakes. Accordingly, I have developed quite a few tools for efficiency over the years. Many of these are elaborated on in greater detail throughout this book. These include:

1. Don't run out of cash.

2. Don't procrastinate—give it away instead (delegate).

3. Admit your own mistakes.

4. Praise others.

5. Make a budget and stick to it.

6. Emotion can trump intellect.

7. Wait three days (calm down before you act).

There are many more, and the rules exist for good reason. Making and following rules for yourself will reduce the amount of time you have to spend correcting your course and will significantly improve your efficiency. And, as you go, be sure to adapt the rules to changing circumstances. Create new ones that work for you, and discard those that have become outdated or no longer make sense.

I often write on Sunday evenings. In case inspiration fails, I have a long list of potential topics I keep on a computer file. I just scan the list, and voilà! A great topic leaps out at me.

But not this time. You'll never guess what happened to that computer file. Neither can I.

From now on I will keep a duplicate of all files.

I promise.

THE MAGIC PIANO

I think that cars today are almost the exact equivalent of the great Gothic cathedrals: I mean the supreme creation of an era, conceived with passion by unknown artists, and consumed in image if not in usage by a whole population which appropriates them as a purely magical object.

—ROLAND BARTHES SYRUS
Mythologies

Make no little plans; they have no magic to stir men's blood.

—DANIEL HUDSON BURNHAM
Attributed

Years ago I owned, along with one of my law partners and my brother, a cabin in the woods at Lake Arrowhead near Los Angeles. One of our first purchases was a player piano. Put in a paper roll and the keys would dance and the music played.

One day Kevin, the four-year-old son of my law partner, visited our cabin for the first time. I started a piano roll for him.

As soon as the music began Kevin's eyes grew wide. He heard the piano playing, looked at the white and black keys racing wildly up and down, and said to me, "A magic piano. The kids at school are never going to believe this!"

I have experienced many moments of magic in my life—moments as simple as taking a deep breath of pine-scented air in a quiet forest, or leaving my office with a profound sigh at the end of a productive day. Moments as stirring as an evening on Broadway when Bernadette Peters seemed to sing "Send in the Clowns" directly to me. Moments as special as seeing my first daughter carried from the delivery room, or seeing my youngest daughter married recently on a hillside in Marin County.

As he sat on the small bench in front of the Magic Piano, Kevin experienced enchantment. What four-year-old doesn't? And what fifty-year-old still does? There is a line in one of my favorite poems, "Anyone Lived in a Pretty How Town" by e. e. cummings: "and down they forgot as up they grew."

But you don't have to forget. That is the essence of this tool. I'm still amazed each time I see a Boeing 747 take off. The first 747 I ever saw nosed to the gate at LAX, and my brother David, a perennial kid himself, said, "It's so big because it carries really big people." We laughed and, amazingly, the first folks off the plane (no doubt because they were traveling first class) were literally giants—the New York Knicks. My brother David never forgot to find the magic in all things. He held on to this gift his entire life.

The magic moments are out there, and within you, all of them, all of the time. That is why I suggest you use the tool of the Magic Piano, so you can experience magic whenever you wish, whether at Disneyland or at work. There is no time or age limit.

Your life is filled with magic right now: the miracle of the Internet, your dog greeting you at home tonight, or a love letter to a friend (which you can write today). I received a love letter from a friend named Sue when I was sixteen and carried it in my wallet for more than fifty years—as a constant reminder of the magic. Five years ago I danced with Sue once again on her 65th birthday.

When you open your eyes, your imagination, and your heart, those moments will find you, and fill you with dreams, which are not so impossible after all.

It's easy to fall into the trap of thinking that a job isn't any fun and that magic can only happen outside of work. I spend more hours at work than I do anywhere else, and I encourage you to think of business as filled with all kinds of magic. Concluding a successful deal is magic, mentoring others is magic, as is working with someone you respect and admire.

I have experienced many moments of magic in my business life, from opening my law offices and working twenty-two days straight, to buying nine rental houses on the same day and depositing an $8,000,000 check at a bank (which had previously turned me down for a $35,000 loan). I've had moments as fulfilling as having a publisher accept my first book, which I had been working on for more than twenty years. And moments as exciting as the day when my first legal secretary told me she had passed the bar exam herself. And when I left my office recently I realized that because I owned the building I was actually riding in my own real, grown-up elevator. Magic.

Being a valued member of a team is magic. A friend's long-term employee told him recently that she had inherited a lot of money.

"I'm happy for you," he said, "but I don't want to lose you."

"Don't tell anyone," she said, "and I won't tell either. I just want to go on being part of the team. I don't want that to change."

Together with four-year-old Kevin, I am astonished by Magic Pianos everywhere I go. I encourage you to use the tool of Magic Piano in your own life and work. Then you too can say, "The kids at school are never going to believe this!"

READY, SET, IMPROVISE

O! How this spring of love resembleth
The uncertain glory of an April day!

—WILLIAM SHAKESPEARE
The Two Gentlemen of Verona

Life's uncertain voyage.

—WILLIAM SHAKESPEARE
Timon of Athens

When I drive my car I sometimes marvel at all of the adjustments a driver needs to make, split second by split second. We watch carefully, listen, adjust our course to stay in the same lane, change lanes, stop for traffic signals, and avoid hitting pedestrians. As I tell my children, if you daydream at the office for fifteen minutes, no big deal. If you daydream for five seconds while driving a car you could be dead. Whenever I drive I pay strict attention.

Driving a car, living your life, or running your business are all entirely based on Ready, Set, Improvise. This is an indispensable tool because to succeed you always have to be ready to improvise. There are physical, social, and psychological guidelines in life, but there certainly is no script. Even when you know what the scene will be, such as an employee review, appearing in court, or asking someone you love to marry you, you can only practice your opening lines. You don't know how the boss, the judge, or your intended will respond, and there are so many possibilities that it's impossible to prepare your own responses in advance. But isn't that part of why we look forward to waking up tomorrow morning? To find out what will happen.

I remember my brother David who appeared in the final round of the Stanford Law School moot court competition. David was arguing his case when Justice Brennan from the United States Supreme Court, acting as the chief judge in the moot court finals, asked him a question.

David looked up at Justice Brennan on the bench and said, "Your honor. I don't know what you mean by that question." The audience gasped. The auditorium fell silent. I was sitting in the front row and hoped that Justice Brennan didn't know I was David's brother. Attorneys have been held in contempt for lesser breaches of decorum.

Brennan adjusted his spectacles and peered down at David.

"Counsel, I don't know what you mean by that answer."

The audience hesitated, then laughed. David must have replied with something really clever, because he won the competition with the unanimous first-place vote of all three judges. David went on to become an outstanding trial attorney. He was always very quick with an answer or a quip.

A friend of mine who acted in the Second City improv company in Chicago disclosed that the most important principle of improv is to respond "Yes, and . . . " rather than "No," because "No" stops the action.

"Let's go to the Chinese restaurant."

"No."

End of improv.

In high school I was a member of the speech club. Our teacher, L. Day Hanks, taught us an important principle of salesmanship: continuous assent. In other words, agree with the other person, then continue.

"I would like a ten percent raise."

"Ten percent? That's pretty high."

"Yes it is. And let me tell you why I'm worth it . . . "

I asked Susan, who later became my second wife, to join me in Hawaii for a week-long vacation.

"I'm sorry," she said, "but I don't have time to plan the trip."

"Yes, I know you're busy, so I'll do the planning. Air reservations, a car, hotels, everything."

"You will?"

"Yes. And I may miss a few highpoints on a vacation, but I've always enjoyed myself."

"Oh. Okay. I'll go."

Call it "Yes, and," or call it "continuous assent." For me life moves forward and each scene concludes most productively when I respond positively to whatever life brings.

As Dale Carnegie, author of *How to Win Friends and Influence People,* wrote in his book *How to Stop Worrying and Start Living*:

"When fate hands you a lemon, make lemonade."

Life is an improv. So is business. Go for it—sugar, lemons, and all.

PEOPLE TOOL 27 FOR BUSINESS

THE TICKER TAPE

The unconscious is not just evil by nature, it is also the source of the highest good: not only dark but also light, not only bestial, semihuman, and demonic but superhuman, spiritual, and, in the classical sense of the word, "divine."
— CARL GUSTAV JUNG
The Practice of Psychotherapy

I believe that in the end the truth will conquer.
— JOHN WYCLIFFE, STATEMENT TO THE DUKE OF LANCASTER
A Short History of the English People by J.R. Green

The unconscious mind is an extremely useful tool, though difficult to access. It is largely invisible, which means that each of us is, at least in part, "an invisible man." How is it possible not to be? I have so many thoughts and feelings that it is impossible for me to convey all that passes through my mind. This is universally true for all of us.

But I am also selective. That is a polite way to say that I edit what I am going to say before I say it. If I think that you will dislike certain words or ideas I will trim my speech to suit your taste. I will censor myself in an attempt to avoid your disapproval. (And, of course, there are certain topics, which "nice" people simply don't talk about.)

All of this is perfectly normal, especially in business. But occasionally I want something which might slip away from me forever unless I act immediately and make myself completely visible. This was the case when I first met my wife Daveen more than thirty-five years ago. In the 2011 movie *We Bought a Zoo* the leading man, Matt Damon, advises his son that to woo and win his lady-love he needed "twenty seconds of insane courage."

That is exactly what I needed to woo and win Daveen.

Daveen was working at a rare bookstore. I was a customer. One day she caught my eye while I was discussing a rare book with the owner. I don't know if you believe (as I do) in love at first sight but I knew instantly that she was the one for me so I worked up the courage to ask her out to lunch.

As soon as we were seated Daveen said, "I can only think of two reasons why you asked me to lunch. First, to offer me a job. Second, you want to date me. Which is it? Because I don't date customers."

Daveen was, and is, clear and straightforward. I am often less direct.

"Well," I said, "I don't need anyone else at my office right now."

Not subtle. Daveen began to rise, and I didn't think she was headed to the ladies room. I knew if I didn't act decisively and immediately in that moment she would leave and I might lose her forever.

"Wait a minute," I said. "We're here, so why not enjoy our lunch. I'll tell you exactly what I have in mind."

She hesitated. On the spot I invented the tool of Ticker Tape. I just blurted out whatever came into my conscious mind. No holding back, no censoring. The game was almost over, and there was a significant chance I might lose her if I didn't act instantly. "Give it a shot," I thought. So I spoke from my heart.

"I do want to date you, and at this lunch I'm going to try to persuade you to go out with me. And I'll tell you right up front that, when I try, I can be extremely persuasive."

I don't remember what I said next. It was probably mushy and might have been embarrassing to me if I had thought about it in advance, but I didn't. I just kept talking. Daveen sat down. She appeared to be interested. The more I talked, the more interested she became. She stayed for lunch. And when my Ticker Tape monologue was over, we talked.

At the end of our lunch Daveen agreed to join me on our first real date—a weekend in Las Vegas.

So when you're really stuck and have nothing to lose, just blurt it out as honestly and sincerely as you can.

In business I suggest you use this tool selectively. But when you are backed into a corner and are going to lose the deal, or the sale, or the client, why be complacent? Act immediately and try the one best option you have left. Speak from your heart. Say what you need to say in a stream of consciousness series of truths. At worst you might not get what you want. At best, you just might be able to turn the situation around. At the very least, why not try?

Ticker Tape. It worked for me. I won the prize. And now I think my wife appreciates that People Tool as much as I do. But I have also used it in business with great success. Maybe you'll "Ticker Tape" your way into the next promotion or job offer.

APPRECIATE AN AUDIENCE OF ONE

If for the sake of a crowded audience you do wish to hold a lecture, your ambition is no laudable one, and at least avoid all citations from the poets, for to quote them argues feeble industry.

—HIPPOCRATES
Precepts

A journey of a thousand miles must begin with a single step.

—LAO-TZU
The Way of Lao-tzu

I recently appeared at a *People Tools* book signing on a rainy evening in Santa Monica. There were far fewer people in the audience than I had hoped would be there. Frank, the event manager, explained that since the bookstore was on the Third Street Promenade, rain kept shoppers at home. We Californians are used to nice weather most of the time and, like L. Frank Baum's Wicked Witch of the West, we melt when we are wet.

My first reaction was disappointment. But then I remembered my story-telling days years earlier. Sometimes the audience was thirty, but more often it was only three or four. Back then I was personally offended when the audience was small, although with time I learned that there were advantages to a small audience. I had an opportunity to establish a much greater intimacy and rapport with everyone there.

After waiting for fifteen minutes, with no more chairs occupied except those by four additional friends who were willing to defy the downpour, I began. Instead of standing behind the podium, I pulled my chair over and sat five feet in front of the small audience who had braved the rain to hear me. A very small audience. All right, other than a dozen friends, my audience was exactly one. I'm good with numbers. I can figure these things out.

I recalled the year when I was divorced from my first wife and regularly picked up my three children for weekend outings. They were ages four, seven, and eight, at the time, and all three were always available and excited to spend time with me. But as they grew up, the oldest found friends and activities that were, understandably, more important than seeing another track meet or air show with her dad. So then there were only two children with me on weekends, and soon enough only one. For a few months I was sad, primarily about being unable to love all of my children with a single visit, but as a result I got to know the youngest far better, and I began to see the alone time with him as an opportunity.

I've built my commercial real estate company over the past forty-five years, and now I'm at the very top in that industry. As an author, however, like every new author, I realize that I am starting at the bottom. I accept radio interviews at 5:00 a.m. and book signings at every bookstore that will have me, large or small. A friend of mine, who has been successfully selling the children's book *The Jester Has Lost His Jingle* for more than eighteen years, told me, "Today you've got to sell books one at a time."

When I started out in real estate I did not have seven hundred investors. I had only one. When I began to publish my literary magazine *Rattle*, it started with a poetry writing class (so there was an entire audience of fifteen). My family foundation took five years to really start making a difference.

Appreciate an Audience of One is a tool that helps you wring great value from time spent with just a few other people, and especially just one. In business, and in life, isn't that always the most important audience you can have? The audience before you? My wife, Daveen, was my audience of one at lunch more than thirty-five years ago. At a well-attended book signing event in Denver an older man asked me to sign his copy of *People Tools*. He said, "I think I'm going to have a very bad diagnosis soon. I hope your book will help." We talked for several minutes and I told him that my mother survived a "you have three months to live" cancer diagnosis for more than ten years by using positive visualization. The man before me was an audience of one (and I was his).

If you work in sales and have only one lead—that lead is your audience of one. If you are looking for a job and have only one potential employer, that employer is your audience of one. If you work in commercial real estate as I do, and have only one potential investor, that investor is your audience of one. Make the most of your opportunity, however small it may seem at the time.

The one woman at my Santa Monica book signing asked to have her photo taken with me and enthusiastically posted it on Facebook. We have kept in touch, and so far she has purchased two books for friends. There is a line in *The Fantasticks*, one of my favorite plays, that says: "There are no small parts. There are only small actors."

At the moment, even if I don't know it, you are my audience of one. And I am your audience of one as well.

CATCH THE UP ELEVATOR

We are here just for a spell and then pass on.
So get a few laughs and do the best you can.
Live your life so that whenever you lose it, you are ahead.
—INSCRIBED ON THE WILL ROGERS MEMORIAL BUILDING
IN CLAREMORE, OKLAHOMA

She [Madam Bovary] had that indefinable beauty that comes from happiness, enthusiasm, success—a beauty that is nothing more or less than a harmony of temperament and circumstances.

—GUSTAV FLAUBERT
Madam Bovary

Where did you start your day? Tenth story with a happy view? Ground floor with Starbucks? The basement of gloom? In business and in life I think you should always go for joy and use the tool of Catch the Up Elevator. And you can do it without the cooperation of anyone else in the world. If you want it done right, in this case, do it yourself.

It makes no difference where you start each day because you can always go up from there. Most of my days begin above ground level and end up higher (especially when I get home in the evening to spend time with my wife and family). But every single day I am influenced either from the outside by other people, or from the inside by myself.

Both joy and gloom are contagious. This is particularly true in a business environment. When my wife is cheerful as I wake up, and she usually is, I latch onto her mood and Catch her Up Elevator. But what do I do when my wife just won't cooperate? On those rare occasions when she wakes up in a bad mood, I sympathize, but I don't enter her Down Elevator. To paraphrase the beggar in *Fiddler on the Roof*, "Just because you had a bad night, why should I suffer?"

I also find that my own mood is infectious—notably to me, and I can infect myself with either a happy or a grumpy face. This is entirely my choice. Years ago I was arguing with my girlfriend Jill when our guest John arrived at our front door for dinner. I greeted him warmly and the three of us enjoyed a lovely evening together. At 11:00 p.m., after John left and the front door had closed behind him, I resumed the argument with Jill exactly where we had left off. She was shocked.

"I thought everything was fine. We had such a nice evening."

Yes, we did, because I had chosen to substitute happy feelings for my previously unhappy frame of mind. Now that our guest had left, I resumed the argument. While John was with us I chose to Catch the Up Elevator. The instant he left I stepped right onto the Down Elevator—both were my choice.

When Daveen and I were married I admitted to her that I had a bad habit. In a prior marriage when I was angry with my wife I would stomp around the house in an overtly bad mood so that she would come after me, trying to talk me out of it. This was my opportunity to suck her in; my misery wanted to grab her company. I asked Daveen to ignore my unpleasant moods. I suggested that she tell me that she would be available when I felt better, and then check back with me in four hours. She has followed my request. This strategy helps me to "get over" whatever it is that is troubling me without dragging Daveen into my basement of gloom.

I always keep my appointments, even though sometimes I am not in the mood. When I put on a happy face to meet a business associate, however, I virtually always feel better at the end of our meeting than I did before it began.

I learned years ago that when I walk into my office wearing a frown, it has an effect on my entire staff. And since everyone at my office accomplishes a lot more when I begin my day with enthusiasm, that is what I choose to do.

As a manager and coworker your mood will definitely trickle down and impact the people you work with. I suggest, for their sake and yours, that you take the initiative every day to Catch the Up Elevator. It will not only improve your mood and the attitude of those working around you. It will also improve your productivity. In fact, I think that Catch the Up Elevator should be an unwritten part of everyone's job description.

Catch the Up Elevator. Ride with joy today. It's entirely up to you.

K.I.S.S.

An old pond—
A frog leaping in—
The sound of water.
—BASHO
After Lofcadio Hearn's translation

Like all Holmes' reasoning the thing seemed simplicity itself
when it was once explained.
—SIR ARTHUR CONAN DOYLE
The Memoirs of Sherlock Holmes

K.I.S.S. stands for the tool of Keep it Simple, Stupid.

When I was sixteen my father bought our first television set. There were thirteen channels, a volume control, and that was it. Simple. Last year, when the cable company I use changed their system from analogue to digital, I spent two hours following their instructions to implement the change. Finally, as a last resort, after another hour on the phone, I insisted that their serviceman make a house call to fix the problem so I could watch my favorite television show that evening.

I am not a car guy. I know how to put the key in the ignition, use the accelerator and brake, and how to steer. When I buy a new car the salesman usually opens the hood and proudly expects me to gush about the beautiful engine. Sometimes I say, "It looks very clean," but I don't really understand a thing about it, other than from a vague memory of how an internal combustion engine might work.

Years ago one of my business partners insisted that the potential investors he was referring to me would not purchase a property unless they knew everything about it. So together we prepared a lengthy document for them to scrutinize. Net result: no investors. I went back to my rather simple two-page presentation, which works. In my experience investors are mostly interested in the cash return on an investment. Of course, if they request additional information I am happy to provide it.

I also discovered, early in my career, that I should present only one investment at a time. When I offered two, my potential investor would always ask, "Which one is better?" I proceeded to patiently explain the virtues and vices of each. The result was a confused investor and no investment.

I have been a licensed C.P.A. I understand numbers. Even so, I believe that a financial statement should ideally be limited to a single page. And if I don't understand the numbers quickly I always assume that either the wizard who prepared the statement was not too competent, or that there is something disturbing which lurks behind the curtain.

A part of simplicity is quality. I mentioned to my son Craig, who wrote the foreword to my first book in the *People Tools* series, that I wanted to write chapters for sixty People Tools for Business for the next book, compared with fifty-four for the first *People Tools*. He said, "Dad, you're falling victim to 'The Presenter's Paradox.'"

"What's that?"

"A presenter often believes that his performance will be better received if he offers greater quantity. He will deliver a forty-minute speech, rather than a twenty-minute speech."

"So what's the paradox, Craig?"

"Research indicates that an audience will evaluate a speech, or your book, based upon the average quality of the chapters and tools, not on the number of them."

"So if I toss out the weaker ones, I end up with a better product?"

"Exactly, Dad. You're one of my better students. Would you like to read the research?"

I thanked Craig and decided that I would include my fifty best business tools in this book.

So let's K.I.S.S. and pay attention to quality. I think my wife would prefer that too.

ASK FOR A
PINEAPPLE FLUFF

Anger is a short madness.

—HORACE
Epistles (First Book of Letters, 20 B.C.)

Anger is one of the sinews of the soul;
he that wants it hath a maimed mind.

—THOMAS FULLER
The Holy State and the Profane State, 1642

For me, and perhaps for you, in both business and in life one of the more difficult emotions to deal with is anger.

My father used to get angry a lot. If he was worried about money he stormed around the house, and the rest of us stayed out of his way. When I asked for something he didn't want to give me, he shouted. When I broke the glass table in the living room . . . well, I won't go further into that.

Earlier in my life as a husband, father, and businessman my actions were strongly influenced by what I had observed while growing up. When I was concerned about money I became upset with my family or my colleagues. When my children asked for something I didn't want to give them, I yelled. And if my business associates crossed my path at the wrong moment . . . well, I wasn't very nice.

Fortunately for my family and my coworkers (and for me) I studied with an outstanding psychiatrist, Paul Ware, many years ago. His approach to dealing with anger was simple.

"We only get angry for one of two reasons," he said. "Either we are not getting something we want, such as appreciation for a rush job well done, or we are getting something we don't want, such as an unjustified letter of complaint."

That made sense to me. And it still does.

Paul continued, "So if someone is angry with me, I tell them they seem angry, and being angry is no fun. I then ask them what I can do right now to help them let go of their anger."

"What if they won't tell you," I asked.

"Good question. Then I say that I want to help, I will remain available, and as soon as they figure it out please let me know."

"What if they want something unreasonable," I asked.

"Then I tell them I can't, or won't, do that, and would appreciate their giving me an alternative."

Several years later I was at the original MGM Grand hotel with my wife, Daveen. This was when they operated a Jai Alai court, which was, for me, a pleasant place to gamble away the evening at a relatively small cost. Each game took twenty or thirty minutes, and there were a number of ways to bet, similar to horse racing.

I always wanted to arrive for the first game, since I was eager to start losing my money. The first evening I was in the casino playing blackjack, and Daveen was supposed to meet me at the elevator on the ground floor at 6:45 p.m. In those days we didn't have the convenience (or intrusion) of cell phones.

I was ten minutes early at the elevator. When the appointed time came, no Daveen. I called up to our room.

"I'll be right down. I'm having a problem with my dress."

"Please hurry. The first game is in fifteen minutes."

"I'm hurrying."

You're way ahead of me, so I won't draw this out. For whatever reason Daveen was twenty minutes late and by that time I was furious.

It was going to be another one of those evenings in which I would sit next to her with smoke coming out of my ears.

But Daveen and I were both studying with Paul Ware. As we entered the Jai Alai facility she said, "I know you're angry, and being angry is unpleasant. What can I do right now to help you let go of your anger?"

What I wanted to say was, "No way, I'll teach you a lesson."

Fortunately, what I actually said was, "I want you to buy me a Pineapple Fluff."

Daveen was baffled. "A Pineapple Fluff?" She was concerned that I wasn't serious. I was. I loved that drink (which I've never seen before or since). I also wanted to set a good example for the next time she was angry with me.

"Yes. A Pineapple Fluff. Large."

"I would love to, darling."

She bought the drink and delivered it to me as I was handicapping the second Jai Alai game.

Daveen smiled, more sweetly than the drink. "You are most welcome," she said. Then she kissed me. Again, I had to set a good example. I kissed her back.

When you are angry with someone in business it will clearly not serve you (or anyone else) to cling to your anger. I suggest you ask the person who has offended you for whatever it is you need to help you let go of your anger or resentment. Make it something that they can deliver (because otherwise the request is futile). And when they do deliver, let go of your anger or resentment and move on. This will serve you and your business well. Holding onto anger and resentment only creates unpleasant and unproductive feelings.

I must admit that, being human, I don't Ask for a Pineapple Fluff all of the time. But when I do, it's not only productive—it's quite delicious.

PEOPLE TOOL
32
FOR BUSINESS

STICK IT OUT

Give us grace and strength to forbear and to persevere . . .
Give us courage and gaiety and the quiet mind,
spare to us our friends, soften to us our enemies.
—ROBERT LOUIS STEVENSON
Prayer

Perseverance is more prevailing than violence; and many
things which cannot be overcome when they are together,
yield themselves up when taken little by little.
—*Plutarch's Lives*, Volume VIII, Sertorius

I recently drove seventy-seven miles north from Los Angeles to attend the first 100th birthday party celebration I have ever been invited to. I stopped at a drug store to buy a card for Bill, the birthday boy. Finding no greeting cards for a 100th birthday, I bought two cards congratulating him on his 50th birthday. The cards were funny and turned out to be a hit.

I have been a guest at Bill's birthday parties for more than twenty years. We used to celebrate at the home of one of his two daughters, but in recent years Bill has lived in a bed, mostly reading or sleeping, in an assisted living facility. He was born in 1914, before the start of World War One, and has been a friend of my father's for more than eighty years. My father will celebrate his own 100th birthday in a few months, and I'm looking forward to mine on March 5, 2040.

Our birthday lunch was in the dining room of the facility. After lunch, Bill's grandson asked, "Bill, how do you live to be 100?"

Bill stared into space. I thought perhaps he hadn't heard or understood the question. All of us waited.

"Stick it out," he finally said.

I thought about how the tool of Stick It Out is often what gets us through our lives.

I thought about the harsh economic times of the past few years—people losing their jobs, their homes, their self-respect. I still recall my own reluctance, for the first time in my life, to go to work and face angry telephone calls and e-mails from investors.

Stick It Out.

I thought about romantic love and its gradual descent from rapture into familiarity, and sometimes into loss and despair. Bill's first wife killed herself after failed back surgery more than fifty years ago. His second wife died more than fifteen years ago after spending years in the solitary haze of Alzheimer's. I stared at Bill's younger daughter. We met when she was six. I introduced her to her first husband when she was sixteen. She now walks with a cane.

Stick It Out.

And yet . . . and yet . . . after the camaraderie of lunch, his grandson pushed Bill, in his wheelchair, back to his tiny room, his bed, and a nurse who delivered one pill.

"What's that for?" Bill asked.

It must have been the nurse's first day on the job. She hesitated. "Dementia," she said.

"What?"

I intervened. "For your memory, Bill. To help your memory."

He refused to take the pill. The nurse left the room to seek either advice or reinforcements. One of Bill's daughters said it was time for all of us to go.

"Thanks for coming," Bill said.

"Bill, it's been a pleasure. Happy birthday. See you at your one-hundred-and-first next year."

Bill smiled.

I rested my right hand on his shoulder. I wanted Bill to feel connected. Too many of us lack anywhere near enough connection with another human being each day, and I like to be complete with those I love, so if we never meet again we are at peace with one another.

"You know," he said to me, "I'm very happy. Through the joys, the tragedies—as Zorba said, 'the full catastrophe.' I'm happy."

Sometimes life is hard. Sometimes business isn't good or marriages fail. Sometimes you don't get the job you wanted or the unthinkable happens and you find yourself having to start over, and the only way forward is to persevere.

I left the room with tears.

Stick it out.

PEOPLE TOOL
33
FOR BUSINESS

THE IMPORTANCE OF TRUTH

Truth is the most valuable thing we have. Let us economize it.
—MARK TWAIN
"Fenimore Cooper's Literary Offenses"

An Honest man's word is as good as his bond.
—MIGUEL DE CERVANTES
Don Quixote, Book IV

What builds in a relationship over years or decades and can be lost in an instant?

A stand-up comedy show in Edinburgh is a strange place for me to receive the best compliment my wife has ever given me. This was not in private, and Daveen was not even talking to me. She was answering a question asked by a comedian in front of an audience of thirty people, four of them dear friends.

The comedian was making fun of the fact that few of us feel pretty, and he pointed to Daveen and asked, "Does your husband ever tell you he thinks you're pretty?"

"Yes," she said, without much hesitation, though you always want to be a little careful when a comedian is running the show.

"And do you believe him?"

"Absolutely. When he says something, he means it." I don't think this is the answer the comedian expected because he seemed surprised, and he stumbled over his comeback. I didn't exactly hear it anyway because my mind was stuck on what Daveen had said.

Gary, my friend and business partner for many years, tells me that I don't take compliments gracefully, and he may be right. But I fully accepted this one. I was reminded of a moment in the movie *As Good As It Gets*, when Jack Nicholson, attempting to persuade Helen Hunt to remain at dinner says, "You make me want to be a better man."

When she replies, "That's maybe the best compliment of my life," Jack shakes his head and says, "Well, maybe I overshot a little because I was aiming just enough to keep you from walking out." My wife, Daveen, will more than keep me at dinner.

But wouldn't it be easy to lie and say, "You look great," because it's convenient? When I was growing up I figured that lying was a good bet. When my father asked me, "Did you practice the piano for an hour today?" I always said, "Yes." I only was punished when I was caught, which was a dismal 80 percent of the time. But sometimes I got away with, shall we say, a little fiction (though I wasn't too smart about it).

When my father bought a new tape recorder I taped half an hour of my piano practice, and played it over and over while I read a book. That was not a good idea. My dad was a professional musician and at the third playing of my "practice" he noticed from his bedroom the identical mistakes repeated in exactly the same order. From that day forward, my piano practices were supervised and I was banned from using the tape recorder.

I thought about this when I started my business and concluded that I didn't have a good enough memory to remember everything I told everyone. So, since I was not equipped to be a successful liar, I decided to always use the tool of telling the truth in order to establish trust. This is an example of how I sometimes make a good decision (tell the truth) for the wrong reason (I don't want to get caught). Although now I have learned the value and importance of not misrepresenting myself, and when I am tempted, I think about the potential consequences.

So as Daveen put it so well, when I say something I mean it. And yes, Daveen, I think you do look beautiful. In black, in red, and in nothing at all.

The answer to the question I started with is trust. It matters in personal relationships, because from trust flows love. Trust is the glue that binds all successful long-term relationships such as the one I've been lucky to have with Daveen for all these years.

But trust is also the essential glue for business relationships. I have been fortunate to have many long-term relationships with a number of close friends and colleagues for more than twenty years. It is these relationships on which much of the success of my business and my life are built. Relationships built on trust flourish, and then life and business flourish as well.

And trust can be easily lost. Once you have established it, work hard to maintain it. One untruth exposed can impact the trust built throughout an entire lifetime and have a devastating effect on your life and on your business. For this reason, I always use this simple tool. When I tell my wife that she looks pretty I want her to wholeheartedly believe me. And when I tell my employees that a potential portfolio sale of half our properties does not threaten their jobs, I know they will believe me as well.

MULTI-GOALING

To do two things at once is to do neither.
—PUBLILIUS SYRUS
Maxim 7

*It is always good
When a man has two irons in the fire.*
—BEAUMONT AND FLETCHER
The Faithful Friends

Efficiency equals earnings. If you, or any of your employees, can become 20 percent more productive, your profit will increase dramatically. That is why I insist that everyone who works for me use two computer screens.

I am dumbfounded, of course, whenever I visit a law office in which the attorneys, paralegals, and assistants have only one computer monitor sitting on their desks. Wake up, attorneys! Don't you realize that for the small cost of one additional screen per desk you can add significant yield to your bottom line? Here I am, writing this chapter on one screen while I conduct research and answer emails on the other. I know that I can have small windows on a single screen, but that feels cramped and it's not as productive for me.

Isaac Asimov, an American author and professor of biochemistry at Boston University, was one of the most prolific writers who ever lived. It is estimated that he wrote more than ninety thousand letters and postcards, which is more than thirty-four a day for fifty years, and published or edited more than five hundred books. He was a lightning-fast typist in the days before computers made the task relatively easy. Isaac Asimov must have been very efficient. In the days of the typewriter I doubt that he ever wrote more than one or two drafts of anything.

You are going to be more productive when you are more efficient. Many people today think that doing two things at once—multitasking—is efficient. I say, "Nonsense."

I can only focus at one task at a time. Like everyone else, I have limited "bandwidth." The trick is not to perform two tasks simultaneously, but to switch rapidly between two tasks. I often answer e-mails while I'm on a conference call, but only if someone else from my office is also on the call so that I won't miss an important point. As soon as I need to participate I re-engage with the call.

But aren't we missing the point when we admire multitasking? I prefer to focus on multi-goaling, which is far more effective than multitasking and is extremely efficient. Consider a sports analogy. A goalie in a hockey game blocks a shot and deflects it to a teammate. With a single action the goalie has achieved at least six goals (yes, that is intended as a pun).

1. He has blocked the shot, which is his primary objective.

2. He has advanced the puck to a teammate, so his team might better score.

3. He has excited the crowd. That's what the audience is paying for. That is why they will buy a ticket to the next game.

4. He has intimidated the other team. It's easier to win when your opponent is discouraged.

5. The goalie feels a sense of personal accomplishment. After the game it's more likely that he will be nicer to his wife and children.

6. He has honed a skill and might earn more money next season.

Boom! Block one goal and accomplish six of your own. I'm not suggesting that the goalie is thinking about anything other than stopping the other team's shot and deflecting it to a teammate, if he can. I do suggest, however, that when you consider your own list of goals you can become far more effective in achieving them by using the tool of multi-goaling.

The ability to multi-goal will help you in life and in business. It is something I do every day. Recently I needed to review a proposal with Yana, who is in charge of investor communications. I knew we would need thirty minutes, so I invited Yana to lunch. In one hour the following occurred:

1. We reviewed the proposal.

2. We revised the proposal.

3. We made a decision.

4. We ate lunch.

5. We enjoyed social time together out of the office.

6. Yana shared a few of her future plans with me.

7. I shared information with her, which will save me time next week.

Multi-goaling works equally well in my personal life. When, for example, I attend a wedding to please my wife, I prefer to enjoy the drive to the event and not grumble (although I sometimes enjoy grumbling). By bringing my iPad with me I can accomplish multiple goals. I can read a book or the *New York Times,* or write a chapter while I wait for the bride to appear. I can also enjoy the celebration and the affection shared by the happy couple. And, of course, I can anticipate and enjoy great food (don't tell the nutritionist I work with) and the companionship of friends I haven't seen for a few years. Once I made a new business contact that led to a profit of $20,000,000.

Maybe I'm strange, but I have enjoyed this Sunday afternoon I spent writing this book. Goals I met are:

1. Having fun.

2. Sharing my business experience with you.

3. Connecting with others on a deeper level than might otherwise be possible. (One author who won the Nobel Prize for Literature was reported to have commented that at times he didn't know what he thought until he wrote it down.)

4. Having three or four nice snacks.

5. Pleasing Daveen, who is happy when I write at home and not at the office.

6. Receiving her great writing suggestions, including the hockey analogy.

7. Occupying my niche—writing.

Each of us has goals. You might, like me, make your goals conscious, and go for more than one at a time.

Meanwhile, I've also been watching the finals of a golf tournament, and Tiger Woods is lining up a chip shot to win first place, and . . .

PEOPLE WITH GOALS USE PEOPLE WITHOUT GOALS

It's them that take advantage that get advantage in this world.
—GEORGE ELIOT
Adam Bede

One man that has a mind and knows it can always beat ten men who haven't and don't.
—GEORGE BERNARD SHAW
The Apple and the Cart

When my mind is occupied, even a cross-country airplane flight of five hours seems short. Otherwise the five hours can seem unendurably long. On one such flight the movies were boring and the canned music dull, so I listened to a speech by a management consultant. One of his statements alone was worth the tedious five hours I spent in my not-so-comfortable economy seat, because it is a very important tool.

"People with goals," he said, "use people without goals."

This is one of those statements that seems both obvious and important the moment you hear it. "People with goals use people without goals."

Suppose we decide to see a movie. I say, "What would you like to see?"

You say, "The new Superman movie. I've really been looking forward to it."

Which movie do we see? The new Superman movie, of course! Why? Because you had a goal and I had none, other than to see a movie with you.

This tool can also double a positive result when people have different goals, provided they are willing to work together to achieve both. Derek, Vice President in charge of sales at my company, interviewed Elizabeth, a potential executive-assistant, who had recently graduated from college with honors and a degree in business. He offered her the job, but during the interview asked Elizabeth where she saw herself professionally in five years. He did not want to lose a new assistant after a month or two.

In rejecting his offer Elizabeth said, "I don't really know what I want to be doing in five years, but I know what it's not: working in sales." Inadvertently, Derek had helped Elizabeth to consider, or reconsider, her goals. Derek, in return, offered to train Elizabeth in sales, but also groom her for a position in any other division in the company if she proved to be a committed and valuable member of his team. "Sales is where it all begins," he said.

Elizabeth accepted the job and asked to work part time in human resources, which she found to be her real goal. Derek was happy to work with Elizabeth and mentor her in sales. Each had goals, and by using each other, each was better able to achieve them.

My Vice President Yana, who is outstanding at investor communications, recently asked to be trained in commercial-property acquisition. I am happy to help her, since my goal is to retain an outstanding coworker, and provide her with as much diverse experience as I can.

My very first legal secretary attended law school and later worked with my company as general counsel.

Setting goals not only helps you to set priorities with others. It also helps you to focus on your highest priorities.

In 1990 I arrived in Oslo to begin a nine-day vacation. It was during a serious recession, and I could not fall asleep in my hotel room. When I can't sleep I either get out of bed and write, or I think about numbers. That night I thought about numbers. Remember that this was in the age of the dinosaurs when portable computers did not fit under airplane seats and iThings were yet to flow from the imagination of a guy named Steve Jobs.

I knew my business was losing a lot of cash each month, and during that uncomfortable night I figured out exactly how much. I couldn't check my numbers until I was back in Los Angeles, so I spent a very long week trying to enjoy Norway. In reading this chapter my wife reminds me that in the morning, before we visited the Kon Tiki museum, I announced that we were cutting back on costs during our trip. We ate cheese sandwiches for lunch.

Back in Los Angeles I was both pleased (because I was correct), and dismayed (because I was correct) when I found that my dismal night-sweat numbers were accurate.

I immediately set a goal to bring cash flow to breakeven within two years. I figured I would have 440 working days to accomplish that, and during each of those days I would have to either increase monthly income or decrease monthly expenses by $341. If you multiply 440 by 341 you will realize why my family and I ate cheese sandwiches in Norway. That's right. My monthly cash loss was a little more than $145,000.

I achieved my goal one month early. I would like to tell you that I never suffered a regular cash loss again. But then I would be deleting from my memory the Great Recession of 2007–2012, and entirely forgetting that Patterns Persist (you will find that tool in the original *People Tools*).

I'm not saying that you have to set a conscious goal for each and every waking moment. Wandering around though your life can yield many unexpected and magical moments. But I am saying that it will be helpful for you to keep in mind what you want to achieve in both your business and your personal life and to establish clear goals. One of my goals is simply that you enjoy this book and use the tools, or your own, to bring greater success and joy into your business and into your life.

ALWAYS RIGHT IS WRONG

How much easier it is to be critical than to be correct.
—BENJAMIN DISRAELI
Speech to House of Commons, 1860

It is better to be vaguely right than precisely wrong.
—H. WILDEN CARR
Economic Journal

"**I**'d rather be right than be president," said Henry Clay, Sr. (1777–1852). He was a lawyer, politician, and skilled orator who represented Kentucky in both the United States Senate and House of Representatives. He was also Secretary of State from 1825 to 1829.

The question in my mind is not whether I would rather be right than president, because who in their right mind would want to be president? (With due respect to anyone who has ever held that office.)

My question is: Would I rather be right, or would I rather succeed? It's the individualist versus the pragmatist. I am the pragmatist.

Many of us, perhaps most, often predict our own failure. "I can't climb that mountain." "My speech will be terrible." "I don't suppose you'd like to go out with me."

So would you rather predict failure ten times and be entirely correct, or would you rather predict success ten times, succeed five times, and be "wrong" in half of your predictions?

I would rather succeed than be "right" about my forecasts of failure.

On November 5, 2013, the *Los Angeles Times* published an article about the orthopedic surgeon Dr. Neal ElAttrache.* He has performed surgery on celebrities such as Kobe Bryant, Arnold Schwarzenegger, and Sylvester Stallone. Tough surgeries. Great results.

His wife asked ElAttrache if he ever got nervous. He said "no," and she asked him "why?"

According to the *LA Times* article, "ElAttrache told her it was because he was always thinking ahead ten steps. 'If this goes wrong, here's what I do. If that goes wrong, I do this.' He always feels confident he can solve the problem."

I am not a surgeon, but I also know that I can solve the problem. I'm not always right, but I am always confident. And I succeed most of the time. Heck, the highest major league career batting average of all time belongs to Ty Cobb. His lifetime batting average was .366 (1905–28). This means that out of 1,000 at bats, Ty Cobb, the best major league batter of all time, failed to get a hit 634 times out of 1,000.

The story, perhaps apocryphal, is told of the Detroit Lion quarterback Bobby Layne, who is reported to have said, "I've never lost a football game. Sometimes my team was behind when the clock ran out."

No one wins all the time, but you are far more likely to succeed if you go into your next interview (or deal or hearing or review) anticipating your own success. Early in my career my partner Harvey and I negotiated for eighteen months to buy an apartment complex. Several times I wanted to give up, but Harvey persisted. After a year and a half the seller finally agreed to accept our offer, and the transaction was later completed. I must admit I learned something— to work hard and expect success. Harvey refused to take "no" for an answer.

Rather than go with Henry Clay, I'd rather concur with Lewis Carroll in *Alice's Adventures in Wonderland*.

---

* Diane Pucin. "Repairing Kobe Bryant, Zack Greinke just another day's work for him," *Los Angeles Times*, November 5, 2013.

"There's no use trying," Alice said: "one *can't* believe impossible things."

"I daresay you haven't had much practice," said the Queen. "When I was your age, I always did it for half an hour a day. Why, sometimes I've believed as many as six impossible things before breakfast."

So why not tell yourself that you can do it, that you will succeed.

Impossible? Not at all. And before breakfast is a good time to be optimistic. Martin Luther King, Jr. had a dream. Henry Clay, Sr. lost his three campaigns for president in 1824, 1832, and 1844.

DELAYED GRATIFICATION

Years ago I was at a comedy show in Inverness, Scotland, and remember one joke which was very funny, but still cuts me to my core.

"I'm on a seafood diet," the comedian said. "I see food, I eat it."

I have always been on the plus side of the scale. When I was ten or eleven my father tried to help me lose a few pounds. We had a running "bet"—lose weight, he paid me; gain weight, I paid him. That arrangement ended when he realized I was manipulating the scale so that I could instantly "lose" between three and five pounds.

My problem, then and now, is that with food, especially salty junk food like potato chips or Cheetos, my brain short-circuits. I see it, I eat it.

The issue is, with food, I never learned until recently the tool of Delayed Gratification.

But with money I am great about this. I always feel safe and secure when I save money. And as you can probably imagine, this has served me extremely well both in my business and in my personal finances.

When I was twenty-three a friend suggested I buy my wife a new dress. I hesitated. "It's not the $20.00 for the dress. It's the $3.00 a year in lost income for the rest of my life. That's a pretty expensive dress." At the time I assumed I could earn 15 percent a year on invested money. My experience tells me this target is unrealistic, but an 8 percent annual return is reasonable. In part I wooed my wife Daveen by exciting her with the idea of compound interest. (Yes, I sometimes take my calculator to bed with us. We call it "financial foreplay.")

To further illustrate this point I offer two examples. At age seven one of my daughters earned $13,000 from saying a single word in a television commercial for Brawny paper towels. If I could invest that money for her at 8 percent until she is 65, she will have $1,223,923.03. That is not a typo. By age sixty-five she will have more than ninety-four times the money that she started with.

Want to be a billionaire? Easy. Invest one dollar at 6 percent for 347 years. If you earn 8 percent it will take only 260 years. But you will need to start when you are very young.

More realistically, if you are thirty and invest $100/month at 6 percent you will accumulate $142,471.03 by age sixty-five. Earn 8 percent and you will have $229,388.25. Start at age twenty and you will own $527,453.99.

At this point you may have grabbed your HP 17 calculator to check out my numbers. More likely, your brain has gone numb. But my point is that Delayed Gratification works with money. Save now and you can spend more, often a lot more, later. But you have to convince yourself that you enjoy the process. No amount of money is worth it if you feel deprived for thirty-five or forty-five years.

And often, especially in business, you need cash. You need to meet a payroll or to forward payroll taxes on time. In commercial real estate you need money to take advantage of opportunities.

But back to Cheetos. For me, Delayed Gratification with food isn't easy. Ask the owner of any buffet restaurant I've raided in the past sixty years. My joy in scarfing down the garlic toast trumps the saying, "A moment on the lips, forever on the hips." Half my body must now consist of potato chips and Cheetos. But it sure seemed like fun at the time.

Delayed Gratification works for business just as it does for individuals. You can save to buy your own office building. Many of the best retailers ultimately realize greater profit from owning their own locations than from their retail sales. And it also works for your time investments. Ed, my Chief Financial Officer, earned both his college degree and his master's degree in real estate while working full time. He gave up many evenings, but he is much more valuable to me and to himself because of his education.

While running my business full time I returned to school for a degree in counseling, and later in professional writing. I have finished this book by working on it evenings and weekends. I did miss many dinners, movies, and sporting events on television. But it has been more than worth it.

I like to save money for the future. I also enjoy learning new skills and sharing what I have learned.

But right now I'm leaving for home. There is an unfinished bag of Cheetos waiting for me in the kitchen.

SOLVE IT FORWARD

Most of the problems a president has to face have their roots in the past.
—HARRY S. TRUMAN
Memoirs Vol. II: Years of Trial and Hope

What we're saying today is that you're either part of the solution or you're part of the problem.
—ELDRIDGE CLEAVER
Speech in 1968

When I was a kid I earned comic book money by pulling dandelions out of the lawn in our backyard. My mother paid me one cent for each dandelion. A comic book cost ten cents. So every week I would find twenty or thirty dandelions to yank out. I liked comic books. One time I wanted to make a lot of money, and I remember talking to my mom in the back yard on a hot Sunday afternoon for more than three hours while I pulled out six hundred dandelions. I think that was the day my mom stopped paying me a dandelion-pulling fee, and I had to locate comic book money elsewhere.

But here is the catch. I only earned a penny if I pulled out the whole dandelion, including the root.

"If you don't pull a weed out with its roots," my mom said, "it will grow back." My mom always checked to see that the long root was dangling from the flower and leaves before I earned my penny.

I learned a valuable lesson while pulling weeds. You have to solve the whole problem, not just part of it.

In my business we have almost three thousand commercial retail tenants. More than 95 percent of them pay their rent in full and on time. Do I send each of them a "thank you" note every month? No. Do I spend my time smiling while I look at the list of everyone who has met her or his obligation at the first of the month? No. But my collections staff and I spend a lot of time communicating with those relatively few lessees who pay late or, even worse, not at all.

In my company, as in most other companies, the Sales department and the Collections department are in a perpetual state of conflict. Why? Because the task of Sales is to sell. A salesman takes the order and immediately moves on to the next customer, saying, in effect, "My duty here is finished. I made the sale."

But it is the task of the Collections department to collect. They don't care very much about sales. So if Sales generates $1,000,000 and Collections only collects $600,000, then Collections will look bad and my entire company will be in trouble.

At my firm we need to lease a substantial number of square feet of retail space every month. We subcontract that leasing chore to an outside group. They are responsible for finding tenants and filling vacancies and they do an excellent job. But our collection problem is tricky because a tenant does not typically default in the first few months. Sometimes a new tenant will pay rent on time for years. By that time Leasing has already collected its commission and moved on. But if we are only able to collect 85 percent of the rent that is due each month, we will soon be out of business.

This is why we insist on checking every prospective tenant's credit and business experience very carefully. Every month we turn down a tenant or two and have an argument with Leasing. The argument goes something like this:

"But that space has been vacant for a year, and this is the first tenant that has shown any interest."

"Right, Leasing, but have you noticed that the prospective tenant will have to spend $25,000 to build-out the store, they have only $5,000 in the bank, and they have absolutely no experience in this type of business?" I hold myself back from discouraging Leasing even further by pointing out that in making an offer for undesirable space the prospective tenant has already demonstrated a certain degree of naiveté.

We (Collections) always win the argument, because "we" is me, and I am not interested in renting to a new tenant who will soon default in paying their rent, and ultimately cost me $10,000 and take four or five months of my time to evict. Of course, we do not always win the war because even though we try to Solve It Forward by renting only to good credit risks, life and the business cycle does intervene.

In effect, I am still yanking out those pesky dandelions. But I always strive to include the roots. When you face a problem, whether in business or in your personal life, solve the entire problem so that it won't grow back. You will save a lot of time, money, and heartache.

In short, don't just solve the problem for the next ten minutes.

Use the tool of Solve It Forward.

007

To Conquer without risk is to triumph without glory.
— PIERRE CORNEILLE
Le Cid

It is only by risking our persons from one hour to another that we live at all. And often enough our faith beforehand in an uncertified result is the only thing that makes the result come true.
— WILLIAM JAMES
The Will to Believe

I would like to be 007—James Bond. This is not some passing fancy. I have wanted to be James Bond ever since I saw him, actually Sean Connery, in the movie *Goldfinger* fifty years ago. I would like to be fit, handsome, and debonair. I would like to rid the world of evildoers. I would like to romp with beautiful women starting, of course, with Pussy Galore (and I have no idea how that name passed the censors).

Of course there is another side to James Bond. He leaps from cliffs or tall buildings. I'm afraid of heights. He is suave. I can't tie a proper Windsor knot. Villains shoot at Bond or try to blow him up. My doctor says I am extremely allergic to bullets, and also to the sight of blood, especially my own.

If Miss Moneypenny called to offer me the 007 job, I would turn her down flat, for the same reason I turned down Daveen several years ago, when she offered to introduce me to Cindy Crawford at a party. While I am perfectly happy to admire Cindy Crawford from a distance, I am shy. And though I think deeply, I do not think especially quickly. Cindy seems quite smart on television, but the thought of trying to engage a celebrity in small talk seems daunting.

While the James Bond fantasy may be confined to my own over-active mind, each of us has fantasies and desires which may exceed our ability, and tolerance for risk, or both.

I don't think I am alone in this. Who doesn't imagine a more exciting or satisfying life? But dreams are extremely fragile outside the womb of the mind.

It is not my lack of ability which locks the cell door on my life as an action hero. I am barred from being James Bond, or saying "hello" to Cindy Crawford, by my own fear of failure and my fear of heights, my fear of the unknown and fear of rejection. But I have to realize that every one of my fears is personal to me, and not universal. Nik Wal-lenda walked on a wire high across a gorge near the Grand Canyon. Christopher Columbus, with three boatloads of men, sailed into unknown seas. People apply for new jobs and are rejected all the time. People start up new business ventures, and they don't always succeed. Either these folks do not share my fears, or they take action anyway.

When I was young I was invited to a wine-tasting party. Even though I was shy and didn't drink wine, I attended the party. The hostess was the only person I knew. I decided to put aside my fear of talking to strangers and resolved in advance to have a series of conversations with as many guests as I could. And I did. I spoke with nineteen strangers before I left that party, and I wasn't rejected once. In fact I made several new business contacts that proved to be extremely useful, and at least one new friend.

Your fears are your own. Many fears you can live with. I'm never going to seriously risk my physical safety. But each of us can modify, eliminate, or ignore a few of our more paralyzing fears. To succeed to your very best potential in business and in life it is imperative that sometimes you put aside your fears and take a calculated risk by using the tool of 007.

Moneypenny, here I come.

ATOMIC CLOCK

An atomic clock is a clock device that uses an electronic transition frequency in the microwave, optical, or ultraviolet region of the electromagnetic spectrum of atoms as a frequency standard for its timekeeping element. Atomic clocks are the most accurate time and frequency standards known, and are used as primary standards for international time distribution services, to control the wave frequency of television broadcasts, and in global navigation satellite systems such as GPS.

—WIKIPEDIA
"Atomic clock"

Better late than never.

—LIVY
History of Rome

I'm sure that my scientific son could explain to me the first quotation above. As a layman, however, I conclude that an atomic clock is the most accurate way we have to keep time. I use the tool of Atomic Clock in two ways:

First, I like to be on time.

Second, I am reliable. I keep my promises.

Since I am far from a real atomic clock, I am not always on time. Since I am human I do not always keep my promises. But I do not intentionally break them.

Ultimately, perception is reality. You are who others think you are. Especially to those who are themselves reliable, your reliability will be an issue.

Many of us shop online. Would you purchase a product if you were uncertain about the reliability or date of delivery?

I still remember ordering cabinets for my home. Delivery was promised in four weeks. After many phone calls and several visits to the shop, I finally received the cabinets six months after I signed the contract. I would never use that vendor again. Can you blame me? Nor would I recommend him to anyone else.

Years ago Marilyn, a close friend of mine, was involved in a bitter divorce. The custody of her three children was one of the issues being decided by the court. When Marilyn's attorney did not return her telephone calls for three days in a row, Marilyn became desperate. She asked for my help.

I took action, and thirty minutes later her attorney called me. He was quite angry because I had left voice messages and sent emails and faxes to his office addressed to him, his receptionist, his partner, his associate, and his office manager.

"Stop bothering my entire office," he said.

"I would be happy to stop. All you have to do is answer Marilyn's phone calls immediately, and I'll never do it again."

After that, he answered her calls promptly.

However, I would never use or recommend that attorney. I judge the quality of a professional's work, in large part, on how promptly he or she returns my calls.

Several years ago I had a persistent, and literal, pain in my neck. I was referred to a surgeon who was highly respected in his field. For my first appointment I waited for three hours in his office. For my second appointment, I waited for two and a half hours. (See *People Tools*, "Patterns Persist.") There was no third appointment.

Several months ago I entirely missed a telephone appointment for an early morning (6:00 a.m.) radio interview. Maybe I just forgot. Or maybe it was a "Freudian slip." I felt embarrassed for days, and was not invited to participate on that show again.

Over the years I have forgotten two lunch appointments. Imagine my mortification in returning to my office at 1:30 p.m. to find a client in my waiting room who had been reading a magazine for an hour.

Two millennia ago Publilius Syrus wrote, "A good reputation is more valuable than money (Maxim 108)." A more helpful thought, also from Publilius Syrus: "It is better *to* learn *late* than *never*." (Emphasis supplied. Maxim 864.)

Be reliable. And always keep your promises.

Atomic Clock. Tick tick.

CUTTING THROUGH THE FOG

Genius . . . means little more than the faculty of perceiving in an unhabitual way.
—WILLIAM JAMES
The Principles of Psychology

I have vision and the rest of the world wears bifocals.
—THE SUNDANCE KID SPEAKING TO BUTCH CASSIDY
Butch Cassidy and the Sundance Kid (1969
Screenplay by William Goldman

As the airplane carrying me from London was on approach to the airport in Palma, Majorca, I looked through my window and was concerned to see that we were landing in a rather heavy fog. But I had confidence in ground radar and our pilots. After we landed safely I looked through another window on the opposite side of the plane to see no fog at all. I looked back through my window. Heavy fog.

Was there fog on my side of the plane and not on the other? No. As it turned out, my window itself was fogged over, creating the illusion that it was in fact foggy outside the airplane. But beyond my window the air was actually clear.

This morning I awoke slightly after sunrise. I stared out the window at faint pink clouds, and the wooden frame of the window seemed to flutter. Was the window frame in fact wavering? No. There was an astigmatism in my eye.

I was struck by the idea that my view of the world is not universal. It is unique to me. I see colors slightly differently than you do. I interpret words in my own way. I like to sit and think. My daughter Sara, on the other hand, likes to keep moving. She teaches yoga for many hours a day. That would not be something I would enjoy doing.

When we use the tool of Cutting Through the Fog we are able to make better decisions and to understand and appreciate the decisions of others. Yesterday I received a draft of six designs for the sign of new shopping center. I really liked version number one, and thought it was far and away the best. I asked several of my business associates which alternative they preferred because I am marketing my center to the public, not to me. Their consensus was either number two or number six. Clearly, my view of the sign, just like my view of the fog, the window, or the benefit of sitting still, was not universal.

Each of us has to remember that our view of the world, in many respects, is unique.

An accountant, a mathematician, and a lawyer were the finalists for the position of university president. The board of trustees arranged for one final boardroom visit with each. The candidate who best answered the same simple question would be hired.

First the trustees called in the CPA and asked, "How much is two plus two?"

"The answer to that question is easy," he said. "The answer is four."

The board thanked him, then brought in the mathematician to answer the same question.

"Well," he said, "to a lay person the answer may seem simple. But to a mathematician, suffice it to say that the answer is somewhere between a theoretical three and a theoretical five."

Finally the lawyer appeared. Before responding he ran to each door and locked it. Then he closed the drapes. Finally he leaned toward the board of trustees and said, "How much do you want it to be?"

In business, and in life, our answers may be simple, theoretical, or whatever we would like them to be. But they will be different.

And this difference, when we embrace it, can serve us well in making decisions. When we open our minds to the differing perspective of others, we will have a better understanding of how they view the world and, as a result, we will make more productive choices. As the French deputy in the back of the chamber shouted out when the speaker noted that there were differences between men and women, "Vive la différence."

I don't speak French, but I echo that statement. "Vive la différence," indeed.

ENERGY LEVERAGE

Greater efficiency equals greater accomplishment.
—ALAN C. FOX
People Tools for Business

What matters most is how well you walk through the fire.
—CHARLES BUKOWSKI
"How Is Your Heart,"
You Get So Alone at Times That It Just Makes Sense

I cannot overstate the advantage of efficiency, in business and in life. In real estate we talk about financial leverage. I once purchased a house for twenty-three thousand dollars with a down payment of one hundred dollars. This gave me the opportunity to earn a very high percentage return on my investment.

I also employ energy leverage. This means that I spend the least amount of time and effort necessary to achieve the maximum result.

Like many people, I simply don't have enough time or energy in the day to accomplish everything I would like to complete. I have developed the tool of Energy Leverage over many years of learning what matters most to me.

At work I focus my attention on those issues that will make the biggest difference in my business. But how do I know what is most important for me to focus on? The answer is simple. I look at those factors that have the largest impact on my bottom line. To illustrate this tool in action I offer a concrete example:

I manage a large portfolio of shopping centers. My goal is to earn maximum cash flow and to increase value as much as I can. Ten years ago I was browsing through statistics from my business when one particular number caught my eye. Our renewal rate on leases was sixty percent. I knew that the industry standard was seventy-five percent. We were falling short of the industry standard by fifteen percent.

What did that single number—fifteen percent—cost? Suppose the leases for one million square feet of retail space expire each year, and that we unnecessarily lose our tenants in fifteen percent of that space. This equals 150,000 square feet of unnecessary vacant space every year.

Let's assume the average rent is $20 per square foot each year, and that each vacant space loses, on average, one year's rent. That's a cost of $20 for each vacant square foot.

Add the cost of commissions to lease the space—about $7 per square foot—and also a cost of $20 per square foot for tenant improvements. That's another $27. So ultimately each square foot we fail to renew costs $47 dollars.

The total annual loss of $47 times 150,000 square feet is $7,050,000. That's right. It's a lot of money. Over a period of ten years that fifteen percent would amount to more than $70 million.

When I discovered this I immediately began to focus my time and energy on carefully looking at all renewals. I still do, and I also make sure that all of our leasing agents have the support they need to maximize our renewal rate. By focusing my time and energy on just this one aspect of my business I have saved my investors (and myself) a huge amount of money.

What else is important in my business? Rent levels. That is another area I on which I focus my time and attention.

Suppose that we rent fifteen hundred square feet for $20 per square foot when we could have obtained $25. That is an annual shortfall of $7,500 (1,500 square feet times $5). But the value of the property would increase by fourteen times the lost rent. That's $105,000.

Multiply that number by twenty small tenants a year and the annual loss in value is $2,100,000. This number certainly attracts my attention. And that is why I follow the commercial rental market very carefully and take the time to speak personally with each of our many leasing brokers every two weeks. I want to rent space at market rents, and not lower, so I support and educate my team to help them achieve this goal.

You don't have to understand the math here. You do have to understand what is important in your own business and in your own life so you can use your own time and energy most efficiently.

There are other rules I follow in connection with the tool of Energy Leverage.

1. *Skip it.* I read carefully through anything that has relevance to my life or my business. If it isn't relevant I skip it.

2. *Establish deadlines.* Give yourself a deadline. I work far more efficiently when I know I have to complete a task by a certain date and time. I also give others a deadline. That way I don't have to follow through as closely. I expect deadlines to be met.

3. *When in doubt, leave it out.* Be succinct. You don't want to read or write any more words than necessary.

4. *Be clear.* When you are clear you will receive fewer questions and leave less room for errors.

5. *Stand at meetings.* They don't last as long.

6. *Insist on reliability.* I don't want to take my car into the shop every month. I don't want to deal with people who change their mind often or have a tenuous grasp on either the facts or the truth.

7. *Value long-term relationships.* I want to minimize the intricacies of dealing with a new individual or company. Many of my employees have been with me for more than twenty years. Many of my investors have been with me for more than forty years. I spend less time

supervising a known employee or contractor, or inter-acting with a long-term investor.

8. *Innovate.* I can research most subjects in minutes on my computer. I accomplish more using two computer monitors.

9. *Delegate.* This is discussed in the chapter on tool #18, "Give It Away." Nothing is more efficient than having someone else complete an entire task for you, provided they will do it effectively.

10. *Educate.* The more you know the less time you will spend consulting experts and the more effective your questions and decisions will be. The more your cowork-ers know the greater number of decisions can be made at their level.

11. *Repeat what works.* Getting ahead of the learning curve always improves efficiency. When I know the layout of my favorite grocery store I can shop more quickly. Ralph's recently changed the location of many products at my neighborhood store. Ouch!

12. *Do it immediately.* There is a cost to look at the same matter twice. Also, procrastination often takes time to explain.

13. *Multi-goal.* This is discussed in another chapter.

14. *Prioritize.* Focus on what matters most. Deal with the most important challenges first.

15. *Create procedures.* If a task will be repeated many times, establish a procedure, preferably in writing. There is no need to reinvent the wheel. Established procedures reduce errors.

I'm sure you can come up with a personalized set of rules that will contribute to your own efficiency. In the interest of being efficient myself, I suggest you do exactly that.

BE PREPARED

Victorious warriors win first and then go to war,
while defeated warriors go to war first and then seek to win.

—SUN-TZU
The Art of War

Be prepared! That's the Boy Scout's marching song.

—TOM LEHRER
"Be Prepared"

You might remember "Be Prepared" as a mission statement from The Boy Scouts of America, or as the title and lyrics of a song by musical satirist Tom Lehrer, or the song by Elton John and Tim Rice from Disney's *The Lion King*, but please pay attention to it. I don't know of any substitute for the tool of Be Prepared.

Recently I read a story in the *Los Angeles Times* about the Wilshire Grand Tower, a new mixed-use building under construction in downtown Los Angeles. When completed it will be the tallest building in the western United States. The foundation alone required the largest single pour of cement for any building ever constructed in this country. Seven separate plants prepared the cement, which was delivered by more than one hundred trucks. Streets were blocked off. The ambient temperature could not exceed a certain level during the days after the pour so the cement would properly cure. In short, there was a tremendous amount of preparation just to pour the concrete foundation. The entire project will take four years to complete. I would guess that my entire office building of 13,500 square feet isn't large enough to even hold the plans for the Wilshire Grand Tower. That is a mind-boggling amount of preparation.

But just as you wouldn't begin to build a structure of any significant size without a set of plans, you shouldn't expect to build a successful career or life without preparation.

"I never prepared for my career," you might say. "It just happened."

I respectfully disagree. You began to prepare for your career when you were born. You have been a student your entire life, whether formally in a class, or informally just by living your life.

For one thing, you learned a language. For another, you learned how to read. Think about it. You are looking at black marks on a piece of paper or on a screen. Somehow those black marks mean something to you. You remember ideas, often because you simply looked at black marks. If you had never learned the language in which this book is presented these same black marks would mean nothing to you. My granddaughter is a fluent speaker and reader of Mandarin Chinese. If this book is ever translated into that language I won't understand a single thought in it. I am not prepared for a career based upon any language other than English, and there are many other careers I am not prepared for. But, as you might expect, for my career I am well prepared. I know the numbers and formulas and codes and regulations and, believe me, they are growing more complex every single day.

It hasn't always been that way. I missed the day in class when our teacher presented the concept of "carrying" in addition. The next day I was in school for the exam. I was asked to add 19 and 13. Simple. Right? You can probably do that in your head. But my preparation for that simple task was missing. I knew that 9 plus 3 was 12, but I didn't know which number I should write down, the 1 or the 2, and which one I should carry. I decided that I should carry the larger of the two numbers, so I wrote down "1" and carried the "2." My answer was that 19 plus 13 equals 41. Go figure! I wasn't prepared.

Since every new day is an improv, you have no choice but to rely on whatever preparation you have made in all of those days past. But can you prepare for tomorrow when you don't always know what is going to happen? Of course. If you set goals for yourself or if you have dreams of achieving something, then by all means . . . prepare! Your opportunity for success increases with your level of preparation.

I delivered a commencement address in May 2014. I wanted to make it as good as I possibly could. Even though I did a lot of public speaking in high school and college, I had never addressed an audience of almost one thousand. I worked with a voice coach for several weeks before the speech. I also practiced my speech every day for two weeks. I was well prepared.

But we also have to recognize that Be Prepared, like any other tool or technique, can be overdone. If I could spend unlimited hours writing, rewriting, and practicing a speech, at some point it might start to get worse, rather than better. And, like you, I have to allocate my time since I don't have enough time for everything. To me, perfecting a speech is only worth the time I can spend on it, and no more. Be ready, but don't overdo it.

Be Prepared. Whenever I see that phrase, the lyrics of Tom Lehrer prance in my head. It's a funny song, but also an extremely valuable People Tool. Use it in your business and in your life and you are far more likely to successfully reach your goals.

CANDY IS DANDY

The story is told of two candy stores located directly across the street from an elementary school. One store prospered. The other store failed.

When a young customer entered the first store and asked for a quarter pound of candy, the salesperson behind the counter was trained to place a small amount of candy on the scale, and then add to it. At the second store the person behind the counter put a larger amount of candy on the scale, then removed enough to reach a quarter pound. The children thought they were receiving more candy at the first store. Not surprisingly, the second store eventually closed its doors.

To be successful, you must employ the tool Candy Is Dandy and pay attention to the perception of others—your vendors, customers, employees, investors, friends, parents, children, spouse . . . in short, everyone.

Value is important. Perceived value is even more important. Early in my career one investor asked me why his cash return was usually greater than what I had projected. I told him I preferred to deliver more than I promised. And for good reason: I wanted my investors to be happy.

My first business was a law partnership. One of the trial attorneys who worked for me consistently promised our clients great results. Even though his performance was excellent, the final result was usually slightly less than predicted and we had many unhappy law clients.

Upon their graduation from college I bought each of my children a new car. One of my daughters complained.

"You bought my brother a car which cost twice as much as the car you bought for me," she said.

"Yes, but your brother paid for half of his car. I only paid for the other half. In fact, I did treat you both equally."

I'm glad my daughter spoke up. Her perception was her reality, and before I explained the situation she felt I had not been fair.

I assume that all of my employees know, or think they know, what others are earning at my company. That can be a problem for morale. I resolve the issue by treating compensation as more than just salary. Flexible hours, bonuses, time off, and other perks are not common knowledge, so no one knows the exact compensation of anyone else and cannot accurately compare.

We all pay attention to value. I suggest that you also pay attention to perceived value and make your candy truly dandy.

STAND UP STRAIGHT

Many receive advice, few profit by it.

—PUBLILIUS SYRUS
Maxim 149

I have found that the best way to give advice to your children is to find out what they want, and then advise them to do it.

—HARRY S. TRUMAN
Television Interview by Edward R. Murrow,
CBS, May 27, 1955

The purpose of the tool Stand Up Straight is to remind us that we should listen to the advice of others. One of the most repetitive bits of advice my parents gave me, and perhaps your parents told you this as well, was to stand up straight. I rebelled. I slouched. What did they know? Of course, I now have spinal stenosis and have been practicing yoga for more than a year so that I can walk for more than one city block without collapsing in pain on the nearest sidewalk or bench.

Learning the tool of Stand Up Straight means that you should listen to advice, regardless of the source, and do what is productive for you and your organization, whether you are the newest employee, the CEO, or, especially, the owner.

I'm afraid that in my life I have ignored a great deal of good advice. My record in stock market investments is dismal. Warren Buffet writes that you should invest only in a company you understand.

I used to consistently ignore him, to the serious detriment of my bank account.

Some good advice I followed. My father told me that if I was willing to make a promise I should be willing to write it down and sign my name to it. One time my business partner Harvey and I were scurrying to put together money for a new investment. We had to rush. I went to my bank while Harvey met my dad at his bank to bring back to me a $6,000 check.

Before my father gave Harvey the cashier's check he said, "Where is the promissory note?"

Harvey was surprised. "This is a loan to Alan, not to me."

"What if you're killed in an auto accident before you get back? What then? How do I get my money back?"

Even though it was a loan to me, Harvey quickly scribbled, and signed, his promise to repay, and then returned to our offices with the check. I did repay my dad's loan. I keep my promises, even if Harvey had to sign for this one.

And just as you might rebel against authority, others may rebel against you. I still remember the most effective lesson I learned in high school. In my senior year my grade in a Latin class hovered between an A and a B. Peter, a classmate of mine, was in the same precarious position. When the final exam was handed back I had scored an A-minus. Peter received a B-plus. I was delighted, and in front of the class blurted to our teacher, "This is great. Now if you give Peter an A you'll have to give me one too."

Our Latin teacher, Mrs. Agulia, responded without hesitation.

"Alan, I don't have to do anything."

My final grade was a B. Peter's was an A.

Thank you, Mrs. Agulia. You taught me an important lesson.

Sic transit gloria. Now I stand up straight, even though my parents told me to.

I'm really still a little kid at heart, and just in case you are too, please keep in mind that I am not telling you to use any particular People Tool. I'm only suggesting that you consider them.

DON'T SING THE "IF ONLY" BLUES

Why, man, he doth bestride the narrow world
Like a colossus; and we petty men
Walk under his huge legs, and peep about
To find ourselves dishonorable graves.
Men at some time are masters of their fates:
The fault, Dear Brutus, is not in our stars,
But in ourselves, that we are underlings.

—WILLIAM SHAKESPEARE
Julius Caesar

Make up your own stories and believe them if you want to.

—MIRIAM WADDINGTON
Driving Home: Poems New and Selected

How many times in your life have you sung the "If Only" blues?

"If only I had won the lottery."

"If only my customer had completed the purchase."

"If only my parents had . . . "

Each of these refrains to the "If Only" blues share one common chord: "The problems in my life are outside of me, and therefore beyond my control."

A companion solo piece is the "Poor Me" symphony for an orchestra of one—you.

"I'm too tired."

"This is too hard for me."

"I don't know how I got into this mess in the first place."

Sometimes I sing these songs too. But when I'm "too tired," I stop, and I give myself a break. When I start driving my car and have a "close call" I pull over and yield the driver's seat to someone else. When I think "it's too hard," I ask for help, give myself a different message such as "I can do this," or I divide the task into smaller portions which are more manageable for me.

I seldom sing the "If Only" blues, but whenever I do I quickly remind myself that, in doing so, I have placed the control of my life in the stars, and not in myself. If my properties are foreclosed I can easily blame the Great Recession. If a valued employee leaves my company I can quickly condemn the job market. If my wife is unhappy with me, well . . . I'm not going to make matters worse by writing about it here. (Just a hint—I'm always wonderful, so she must be crazy to complain.)

When I place the locus of control of my life anywhere but within my own skin, I then have a problem that I cannot possibly solve. I do not control the economy, the job market, or Daveen. If my difficulty comes entirely from outside of me, I am helpless to change the situation. In fact, I am conceding that I have no power to be an agent of change in my own life. And if I can't help myself, well . . . I guess I'll have to buy a lottery ticket to make my fortune, small or large.

Alas, research shows that many of those who win the lottery could write the following letter twelve months later:

Dear Brutus,

One year ago I finally won the lottery—almost five million dollars. But I lost it all to crooks, former friends, and bad stock market advice. I think the fault does lie in our stars. I didn't do anything wrong. I guess I still have enough money to buy a few more lottery tickets.

Very truly yours,
A former multi-millionaire

Each of us is the hero in his or her own story, but the world of humans is a world of tragedy.

Some tragedies, such as earthquakes killing tens of thousands of people, may be beyond our control. Other tragedies, such as war, may be within our control but happen anyway.

To me the real tragedy is that of complacency. As the original gossip columnist Walter Winchell famously remarked, "Nothing recedes like success."

When your business succeeds, life is an endless treat. Although even when you're on a roll, you still don't know what tomorrow may bring. But pay attention to whatever yellow brick road brought you to the cusp of victory. Stay humble, remain vigilant.

And the next time you find yourself singing the "If Only" blues, take a moment to shift the responsibility for solving a problem back to where it belongs. Don't wait for anyone outside of you to solve it for you. This is the best tool you can have to take control of your own life. Why keep on singing the blues when you could be whistling a happy tune instead?

ULTIMATUM

Let us never negotiate out of fear, but let us never fear to negotiate.
—JOHN FITZGERALD KENNEDY
Inaugural address

We live not as we wish to, but as we can.
—MENANDER
Lady of Andros

An "ultimatum" is defined on dictionary.com as "a final, uncompromising demand or set of terms issued by a party to a dispute, the rejection of which may lead to a severance of relations or to the use of force."

Whenever I receive a "my way or the highway" challenge, my first strong impulse is to reject it. Most people react the same way. Beware.

Years ago I worked with Bradley, a real estate developer. He proposed to build a small shopping center on spec. We discussed the project for more than two years. I agreed to put up all of the money and Bradley agreed to split the profit 50-50, which was customary at the time.

One day Bradley visited my office.

"The project is ready to start," he said, "and the profit will go 75 percent to me and 25 percent to you."

"Wait a minute, Brad. For years now we've talked about a 50-50 split. What changed?"

"It looks like the development will be even more successful that I thought, I put it together, and I want 75 percent of the profit."

"But we verbally agreed to 50-50."

"I get 75 percent or I find another investor."

Bradley's ultimatum indicated to me that he had already found another investor, one who would give him 75 percent of the profit.

"Brad, I wish you every success. I'm out." You may have heard similar words from one of the financiers on the TV program "Shark Tank."

I did not shed any tears when I found out several years later that Bradley's project had been lost. During construction, interest rates had soared, "take out" financing was not available, and the property was lost to foreclosure. Bradley spent three years of his life with no profit. His new investor lost whatever money he had put in.

I remember a second ultimatum, which I also refused.

I had purchased a 247-unit apartment complex in Sacramento from Karl, the developer, and I was under contract to purchase the second phase, a 260-unit property, as soon as it was completed. There were construction defects in the first 247 units and the apartment rental market had softened, so I didn't really want to complete my purchase.

Three weeks before the agreed upon closing date of August 15th, I received a threatening letter from Tom. "Close by August 7th," he wrote, "or there is no deal."

I immediately messengered back my response. "You have changed the terms of our agreement, which is an anticipatory breach of contract. I hereby notify you that because of your breach I am terminating the agreement."

In the ensuing litigation Tom testified that he had never received my response, so it was not effective. When he was confronted with the messenger slip signed by someone in his office he harrumphed, "That must have been a temp who signed it. It never got to me."

The court decided that I didn't have to buy the property.

Should you ever issue an ultimatum? Only if you're desperate, really don't care about the outcome, or are nearly certain your ultimatum will work. Of course, you never can be absolutely certain about that (at least not with me). You risk your credibility with the other side, with your own advisors, and with yourself. When you jump off the ultimatum cliff you had better be fully prepared for a hard landing.

Ten years ago I gave a "take it or leave it" demand of my own in a business meeting at my office, simply because I was in a hurry. This is hardly a good reason, but I was quite sure, though not certain, that it would be accepted. I was the executor of my brother David's estate. Before he died, David had hired Merv, a programmer, to create custom software for his business. The programmer had been billing my brother between two and three thousand dollars a month for two years. After David's death the programmer billed $58,000 for his final month of work. That sounded far too high to me.

I was flying from Los Angeles to San Francisco at 2:00 p.m., and I had to leave for the airport. At noon, after a one-hour meeting, I issued an ultimatum, "$25,000. Take it or leave it. This offer is good until 5:00 p.m. today. After that, my offer will be zero. I'll give you my cell phone number." My offer was relatively high, because I knew that litigation would probably cost more than $20,000. Nuisance value, along with every other cost of doing business, or life, seems to increase every year.

The programmer huffed that he had performed the work and wouldn't take less than $35,000. I politely said "no," and excused myself.

At 4:00 p.m. I received a call. "How about $30,000?"

"No. $25,000. 5:00 p.m." He hung up on me.

At two minutes before 5:00 my cell phone rang again. I smiled. "O.K. $25,000."

"You've got a deal. As soon as the paperwork is signed the estate will pay you." I always demand top service and the best price. What I offer in return is immediate payment.

I have given you three examples of Ultimatum. In the first, with the real estate developer, I said "no." In the second, after his ultimatum to me, the seller lost his sale. In the third I was stubborn because I was rushed. The tool of Ultimatum is like dynamite—useful, but only when handled properly.

(Warning: You should never use Ultimatum in your own living room. A spouse or children might be present. I'll explain that difficulty in my next two books: *People Tools for Couples* and *People Tools for Parenting*.)

THE CUSTOMER IS ALWAYS THE CUSTOMER

We heed no instincts but our own.
—JEAN DE LA FONTAINE
Fables

For loveliness
Needs not the foreign aid of ornament,
But is when unadorned adorned the most.
—JAMES THOMPSON
The Seasons

Why is The Customer Is Always the Customer an important tool? Because it holds one of the most important lessons you can learn, not only in this book, but also in life. Every business, and every life, must have customers. If you take away the customers from your local dry cleaner, or Google, or General Motors, then they have no business. If you eliminate everyone else from your world, your friends, family, colleagues, and acquaintances, then you have no life.

If you can only have one skill in life, learning how to effectively work with your customers, in business or in life, is the one to have.

This tool is my answer to the old adage, "the customer is always right." While there's a lot of truth to that statement, in my experience, the customer is NOT always right. For example, a customer who screams at you for five minutes in front of other customers is not likely to win your cooperation. I wouldn't want him or her in my place of business or in my life. When I sell real estate to investors I do not negotiate price. A potential investor who wants a discount is almost certainly right—for him or herself, but not for me. After all, almost everyone wants a bargain. I price fairly, I seek to provide outstanding service, and a lower price would either lead to a reduction in my level of service or a financial loss which might eventually put me out of business.

So let's add some nuance to this old adage. The customer is NOT always right, but the Customer Is Always the Customer, and you must keep their needs and desires in mind for your business to thrive. This means you can't just do what you think is right. Jean de La Fontaine, quoted above, wrote in 1668, "We heed no instincts but our own." I agree. That is our strong tendency. But your own instincts might put you out of business more quickly than an unpaid payroll tax.

In terms of business and the customer, the first example I think of is a restaurant. Restaurants are popular. A large proportion of food consumed in the United States is provided at restaurants. On my way home tonight I bought take-out from a local café. At the shopping centers I manage, more and more tenants are restaurants.

Let's suppose that every time I'm hungry my instincts around food lead me to either a peanut butter and jam sandwich on sourdough French bread or a tuna salad on rye. Following my instincts I might open a sandwich shop where I only serve peanut butter and jam on sourdough French bread or tuna salad on rye. That's it. I drink water, so my instinct might also be to assume that my customers will be exactly like me and drink water, not those appalling soft drinks or, heaven forbid, beer. How long would my restaurant be open?

You're right. I would be in business only until my original cash stake ran out because I would be losing money every single day. I once dined in a French restaurant, which was quite pleasant until the owner flew into a rage when I asked for ketchup for my French fries. As I said, I dined there once.

The Customer Is Always the Customer. I have to please the customer with my location, product, and service. And when I please the customer I will please myself by being successful in terms of sales and profit.

There are many more concerns you should consider before you open a restaurant, or any other business, of your own. However, I implore you to always consider your potential customers first. In this book I'm keeping the chapters about each People Tool for Business as short and interesting as I can. If you become bored you're not going to finish reading this book, and you certainly won't recommend it to a friend.

And, in life, who are the people that are important to you? What can you add to their lives? Can you enjoy a movie together, or a museum, or a meal? Do they fall asleep, as I have, at a four-hour opera? (I'm not slighting opera. I am emphasizing the differences in what we like.)

Without customers (friends, family, colleagues, or acquaintances) you have no business.

Without other people (your customers) you have no life.

The Customer Is Always the Customer.

Now I'm really hungry. It's time for a peanut butter (extra chunky) and jam (apricot) sandwich on sourdough French bread.

APPRECIATION ATTACK

There are but three events in a man's life: birth, life, and death.
He is not conscious of being born, he dies in pain, and he forgets
to live.
— JEAN DE LA BRUYÈRE
Les Caractères

Nowadays we are all of us so hard up that the only pleasant things
to pay are compliments. They're the only things we can pay.

— OSCAR WILDE
Lady Windermere's Fan

While management in business is a serious and goal-directed pursuit, there is a contrary concept I read about years ago—Management by Walking Around. The idea is that sometimes you can manage best just by wandering around the factory floor, or the office, without any specific agenda other than to learn something useful.

I have applied this idea at meetings. Often I learn more of what I should know in the conversations that materialize before and after the actual meeting than I do in the meeting itself. One of our supervisors, Maxine, was assigned to regularly visit our properties in Seattle. Her work was excellent, but she was strictly a nine-to-fiver, whether in the office or on the road. In Seattle, she stopped work at precisely five o'clock and headed for her hotel room. No dinners with her coworkers, no bonus time spent with suppliers. At five o'clock her business day was finished and all professional communication stopped. While I appreciate setting personal boundaries, Maxine was missing a perfect opportunity to build connections and get to know her coworkers better. And in business (just as in life) connections are everything.

When I am on the road the real fun and work begins as day blends into evening. I take advantage of the opportunity to relax, enjoy dinner at a restaurant recommended by my staff, and spend time away from purely commercial concerns. I treat my employees to dinner, a spouse or friend is welcome, and we are often joined by other business associates. This is what I live for—being part of a team, out on the town and having a good time. I always learn more about the people I work with when we unwind together. I find I like them better and appreciate them more as fellow human beings.

Recently, texting has come into vogue. One morning, to my surprise, my iPhone chimed and I found a text from my wife that read, "Love attack. Thinking about you with love in my heart."

Normally I dislike interruptions to my business focus. In this case, however, I had to smile. I felt as if the sun had peeked out from behind a cloud, and warmed me with the unexpected tenderness of Daveen's message.

We all accumulate tidbits from our day to share with somebody later. Daveen was, in effect, saying, "Why wait for later?" and invented the wonderful tool of Appreciation Attack.

Today when I have a happy thought about someone, I take a break from my always "important" work and send them a note.

"I love you back."

"I've enjoyed working with you for thirty years."

"Thanks for getting back to me so quickly."

"It's great to hear from you."

"I'm remembering the thrill we shared last weekend at the soccer game."

"Looking forward to your recital."

"I grin when I think about you."

Oscar Wilde might be smiling, wherever he is.

Why not tell several people right now how much you appreciate them. Both of you will be happier as a result of an Appreciation Attack.

DRIVE WITH CARE

Surgeons must be very careful
When they take the knife!
Underneath their fine incisions
Stirs the Culprit—Life!
—EMILY DICKINSON
No. 108

For tyme ylost may nought recovered be.
—GEOFFREY CHAUCER
Troilus and Criseyde

What does the tool of Drive with Care have to do with business? Everything. If you are in a hospital bed, permanently impaired, or dead, your job or your business will suffer.

When you drive your job or your business with care, each will thrive, and when your job or your business thrive, your coworkers and all those you love will flourish.

When my children were teenagers they asserted their independence, which was natural and necessary. I could no longer effectively tell them what time to go to bed or how often to brush their teeth. But I still hoped I could influence them in just one matter: safe driving. I had told them ever since they were young that if you fall asleep in class your grade may suffer, but that driving is the most dangerous activity that all of us engage in regularly and if you fail to pay attention for even five seconds you could be dead, or worse.

I know that you have lived your own life for many years and that you are somewhat set in your ways, as am I. But I hope that after reading this book you will carry with you and implement at least one simple message—drive your car and your life with care.

I have been careless or, at least, undisciplined in part of my life. When I graduated from high school at age seventeen I weighed 207 pounds. Throughout my life I gradually gained weight. By age seventy I had ballooned to 278 pounds. Gradually my body began to unravel. I could barely pull myself up after I sat on a sofa. My right knee hurt, and it was difficult for me to walk up or down stairs. Finally, I couldn't walk or stand for more than a minute or two without acute pain at the base of my spine. So I decided to be more careful. With the guidance of a specialist I reduced my weight to 210 pounds. The pain in my knee has disappeared. Even though I don't like exercise, last year I began yoga lessons to strengthen my core muscles so that I could walk and stand freely again. Today I'm in good shape for a man of my age. I can stand or walk for as long as I need to. I have been more careful with my life.

In the years 2005 to 2007 my business flourished. I refinanced properties, my bank account swelled. I have always fancied myself to be careful with money, but during that period I invested most of my cash "windfall" in other people's businesses. I also bought three private jets. Within three years most of those investments were gone, and I was fortunate to get back at least part of my money from those few companies which hadn't vanished. In retrospect I realize that I didn't drive my financial life with care.

I don't know how much money I lost in the seven years following 2005. I do know that I don't even want to add it up. I was careless with both my body and my capital.

During the "Great Recession" which, for me, lasted from 2007 until 2012, for the first time in my life I was reluctant to leave for work in the morning. Each evening I asked my wife what day it was because the best night of the week was Friday. At least when I worked on the weekend my telephone didn't ring as much.

The next-to-last tool in my first book, *People Tools*, is Uneven Steps. In it I suggest that we be mindful and pay close attention to each of life's uneven steps. To paraphrase the great 18th century Irish politician John Philpot Curran, "The price of liberty is eternal vigilance."

But perhaps you have a double standard. I know I do.

Waiting at a red traffic signal I am still tempted to take a peek at the messages on my iPhone, and I occasionally yield to that impulse. But if I were sitting behind the driver of a school bus and saw him sneak a peek at his text messages, I would strongly ask him to stop risking the lives of children. I would later report his action to a supervisor. But if, while driving, I glance at my text messages instead of at the road, I don't report myself to anyone.

I will end with a story I will never forget. I hope that you will never forget it either.

Six years ago my younger son Craig was married at a resort, high in the mountains of Malibu. In the afternoon, as Daveen and I drove to the wedding, we both commented on the steep and winding road.

"I'm glad we don't drink," Daveen said. "I would hate to take any chances driving down this road in the dark after the wedding."

I agreed, and we shared a prophetic sigh.

The celebration was high spirited and lasted long into the evening. Craig and his charming bride had invited many friends, including a dozen or so who worked in my office.

After the photographs and the ceremony, after the dancing and the music, after wine and wedding cake were a memory, Daveen and I headed down the mountain on the narrow unlit road. After one sharp left turn we came upon three or four cars parked at the side of the road. We stopped.

"What's wrong?" I said. A group had gathered in the darkness. They were staring down an abyss.

"A car went off the road."

I froze, hoping it wasn't anyone who had attended the wedding.

"Tom is climbing down to take a look."

Mobile phones didn't function in that remote location. As we all began to shiver, he returned.

"There's a car down there. I think there's a body in it. I couldn't tell for sure."

Soon the police arrived and asked us all to leave.

Back on Pacific Coast Highway, with Daveen driving, I used my cell phone to call everyone I knew who had been at the ceremony. Several answered, including my Chief Financial Officer. Several did not. I was concerned.

At two in the morning Daveen and I received the call.

"It was Tammy. Where the road curved left, her car went over the side. The police said she was driving too fast to make the turn."

"Will she be okay?" Sometimes you ask the question even when you know the answer.

Tammy was one of the finest people I have ever worked with. She was the mother of two young children, one with special needs. That night she had passed two cars in the dark, rushing to meet her boyfriend who was waiting for her at her home. Tammy's final photo, taken at the wedding, is today posted in our lunchroom and also rests behind my desk. She appears to be gazing at the stars.

We all live in Kansas, as well as in the astonishing Land of Oz. Please drive carefully on life's steep and winding yellow brick roads— both real and metaphorical. When you conduct your business and your life with care, each will blossom. When both your business and your life bloom, your coworkers, your family, and all around you will be truly alive, with strong hearts and thoughtful minds, and with the courage to persevere and thrive. Then each of us will be fully aware, to share his or her remarkable life.

I hope you have enjoyed this book and will enrich your life with those tools that make sense to you and seem helpful. Let's keep in touch.

ABOUT THE AUTHOR

© Gregg Segal Photography

Alan C. Fox has enjoyed a number of lifetimes during the past seventy-four years. He has earned university degrees in Accounting, Law, Counseling, and Professional Writing. Alan has been employed as a tax supervisor for a national CPA firm, established his own law firm, and founded a commercial real estate company in 1968 that today owns and manages more than seventy major income-producing properties in eleven states.

Alan is also the founder, editor, and publisher of *Rattle*, one of the most respected literary magazines in the United States, and sits on the board of directors of several non-profit foundations.

His successful book, *People Tools: 54 Strategies for Building Relationships, Creating Joy, and Embracing Prosperity* was a *New York Times* best seller in early 2014.

People Tools for Business contains the distillation of Alan's years of experience from working in accounting, law, and real estate. It also includes his deep involvement in poetry, three marriages, and raising six assertive children, two step-children, and one foster child. *People Tools for Business* is Alan's way of sharing with you the benefit of a way of thinking that comes from all of his knowledge, successes, and failures.

Subscribe to a weekly blog for inspiration and insight. Each Tuesday Alan shares additional People Tools, stories, and insights at peopletoolsbook.com.

Contact Alan directly at alan@peopletoolsbook.com

Facebook: PeopleToolsBook

Twitter: @AlanCFox